SUPER EASY SONGBOOK

KIDS' SONGS

T0087275

Technicolor® is the registered trademark of the Technicolor group of companies.

ISBN 978-1-4950-7612-1

7777 W. BLUEMOUND RD. P.O. BOX 13819 MILWAUKEE, WI 53213

Visit Hal Leonard Online at
www.halleonard.com

Welcome to the *Super Easy Songbook* series!

This unique collection will help you play your favorite songs quickly and easily. Here's how it works:

- Play the simplified melody with your right hand. Letter names appear inside each note to assist you.

- There are no key signatures to worry about! If a sharp ♯ or flat ♭ is needed, it is shown beside the note each time.

- There are no page turns, so your hands never have to leave the keyboard.

- If two notes are connected by a tie ‿, hold the first note for the combined number of beats. (The second note does not show a letter name since it is not re-struck.)

- Add basic chords with your left hand using the provided keyboard diagrams. Chord voicings have been carefully chosen to minimize hand movement.

- The left-hand rhythm is up to you, and chord notes can be played together or separately. Be creative!

- If the chords sound muddy, move your left hand an octave* higher. If this gets in the way of playing the melody, move your right hand an octave higher as well.

  * *An octave spans eight notes. If your starting note is C, the next C to the right is an octave higher.*

---------- ALSO AVAILABLE ----------

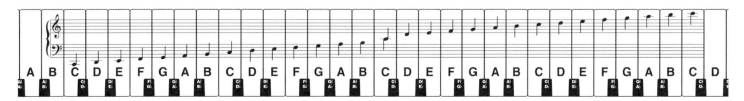

Hal Leonard Student Keyboard Guide HL00296039

Key Stickers HL00100016

Animal Crackers in My Soup
from CURLY TOP

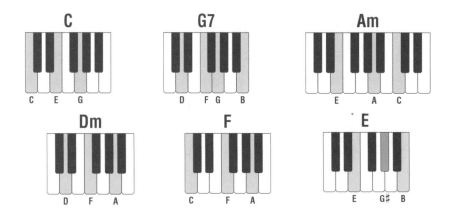

Words by Ted Koehler
and Irving Caesar
Music by Ray Henderson

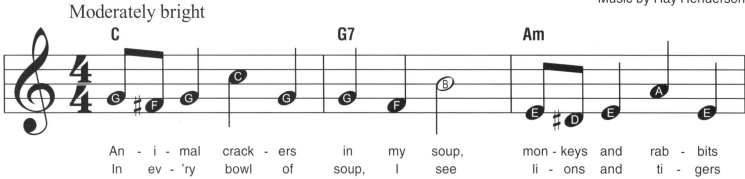

An - i - mal crack - ers in my soup,
In ev - 'ry bowl of soup, I see

mon - keys and rab - bits
li - ons and ti - gers

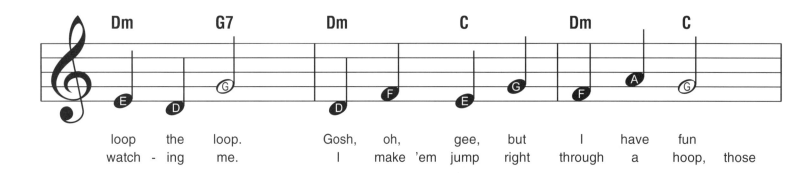

loop the loop.
watch - ing me.

Gosh, oh, gee, but
I make 'em jump right

I have fun
through a hoop, those

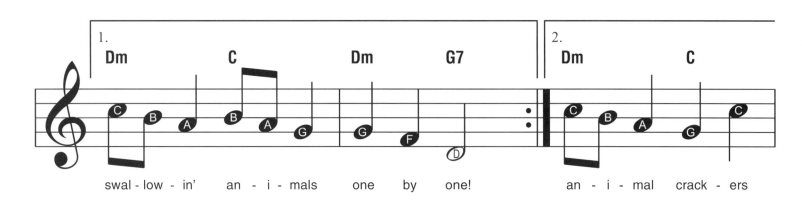

swal - low - in' an - i - mals one by one!

an - i - mal crack - ers

Any Dream Will Do

from JOSEPH AND THE AMAZING TECHNICOLOR® DREAMCOAT

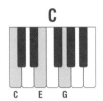

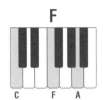
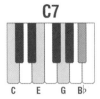
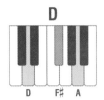

Music by Andrew Lloyd Webber
Lyrics by Tim Rice

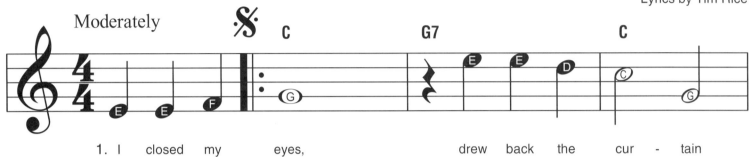

1. I closed my eyes, drew back the cur - tain
(2., 3.) *See additional lyrics*

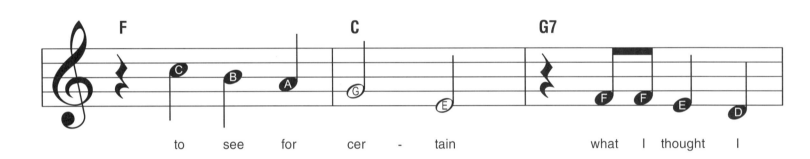

to see for cer - tain what I thought I

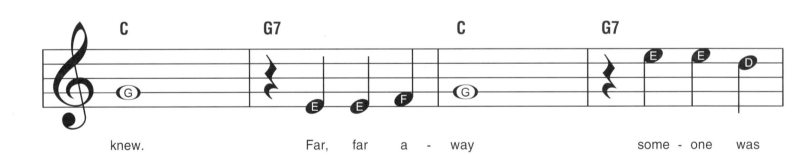

knew. Far, far a - way some - one was

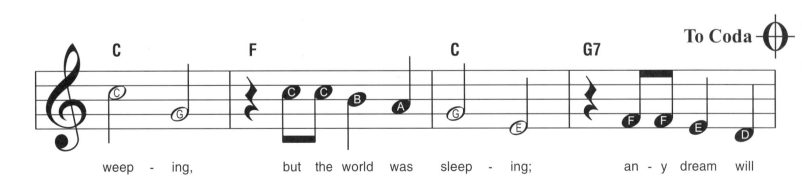

weep - ing, but the world was sleep - ing; an - y dream will

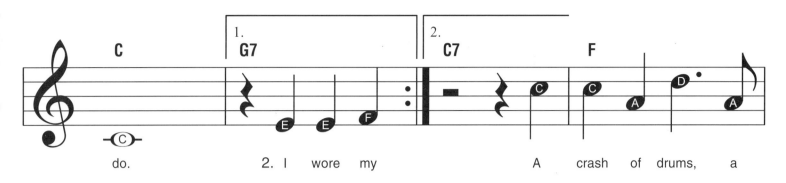

do. 2. I wore my A crash of drums, a

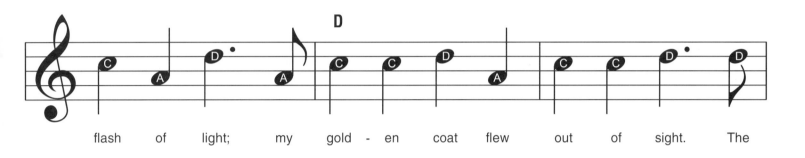

flash of light; my gold - en coat flew out of sight. The

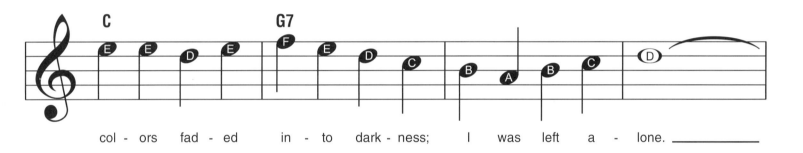

col - ors fad - ed in - to dark - ness; I was left a - lone. _____

D.S. al Coda
(Return to 𝄋, play to ⊕
and skip to Coda)

CODA

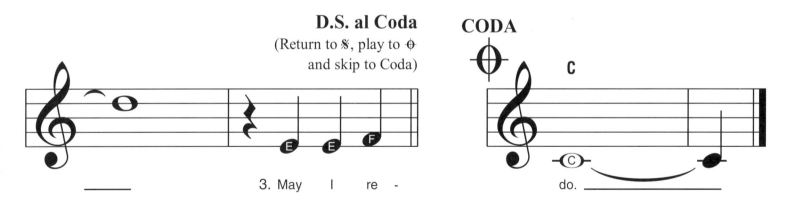

_____ 3. May I re - do. _____

Additional Lyrics

2. I wore my coat with golden lining,
   Bright colors shining, wonderful and new.
   And in the east, the dawn was breaking
   And the world was waking; any dream will do.

3. May I return to the beginning?
   The light is dimming and the dream is, too.
   The world and I, we are still waiting,
   Still hesitating; any dream will do.

"C" Is for Cookie
from the Television Series SESAME STREET

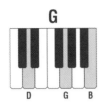
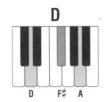
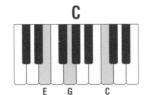
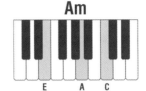

Words and Music by
Joe Raposo

Moderately

C is for cook - ie, that's good e - nough for me!

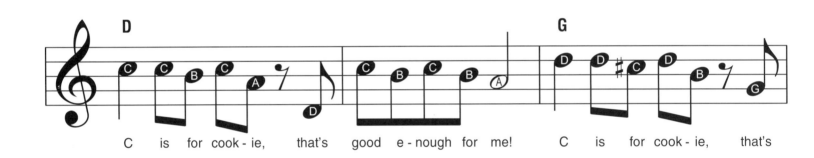

C is for cook - ie, that's good e - nough for me! C is for cook - ie, that's

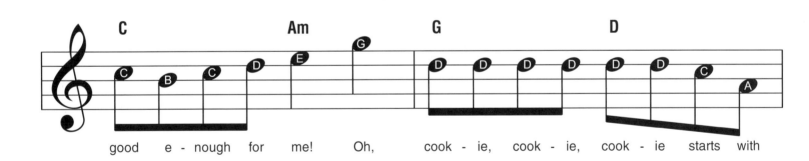

good e - nough for me! Oh, cook - ie, cook - ie, cook - ie starts with

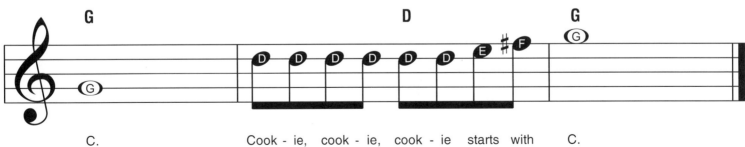

C. Cook - ie, cook - ie, cook - ie starts with C.

The Candy Man
from WILLY WONKA AND THE CHOCOLATE FACTORY

Words and Music by Leslie Bricusse
and Anthony Newley

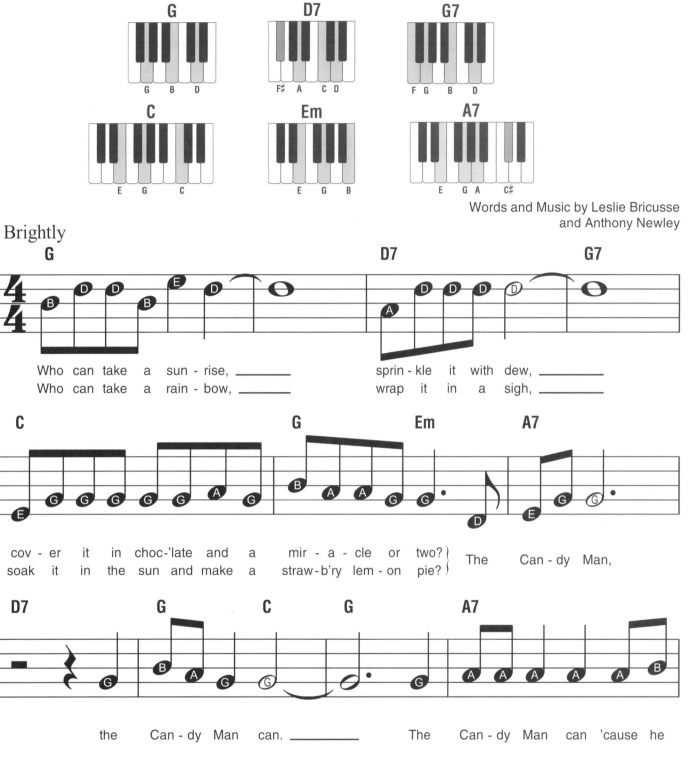

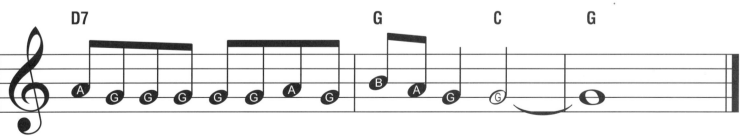

Castle on a Cloud
from LES MISÉRABLES

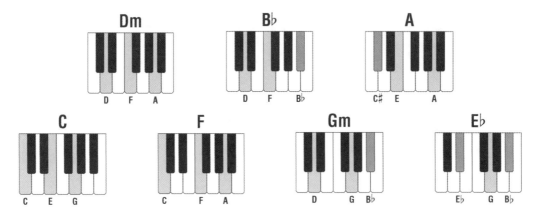

Music by Claude-Michel Schönberg
Lyrics by Alain Boublil,
Jean-Marc Natel and Herbert Kretzmer

Gently

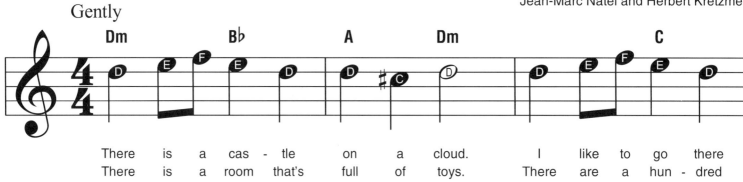

There is a cas - tle on a cloud. I like to go there
There is a room that's full of toys. There are a hun - dred

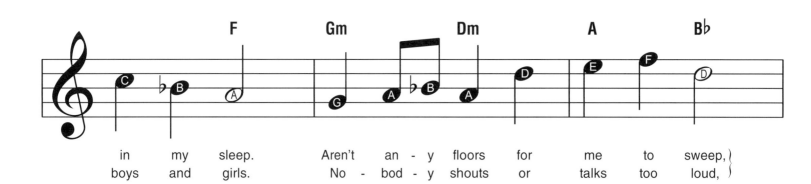

in my sleep. Aren't an - y floors for me to sweep,
boys and girls. No - bod - y shouts or me talks too loud,

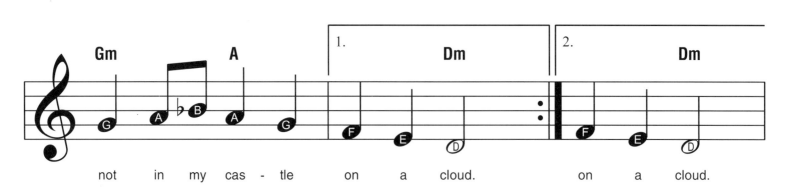

not in my cas - tle on a cloud. on a cloud.

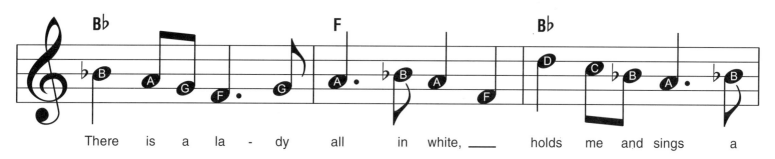

There is a la-dy all in white, ___ holds me and sings a

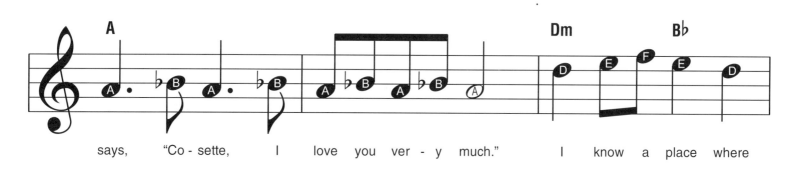

lull - a - by. She's nice to see and she's soft to touch. She

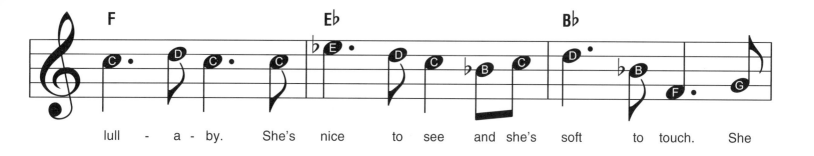

says, "Co - sette, I love you ver - y much." I know a place where

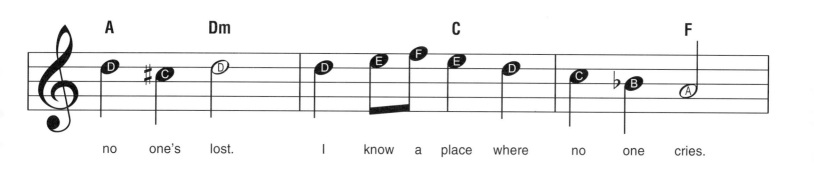

no one's lost. I know a place where no one cries.

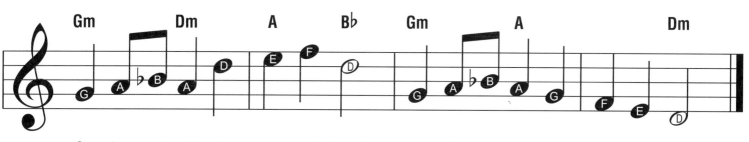

Cry - ing at all is not al - lowed, not in my cas - tle on a cloud.

Chitty Chitty Bang Bang
from CHITTY CHITTY BANG BANG

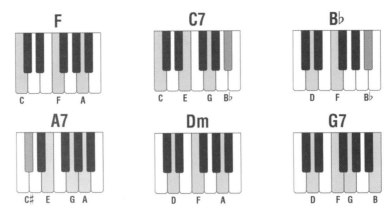

Words and Music by Richard M. Sherman
and Robert B. Sherman

Moderately fast

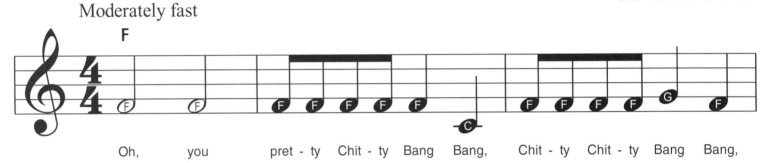

Oh, you pret-ty Chit-ty Bang Bang, Chit-ty Chit-ty Bang Bang,

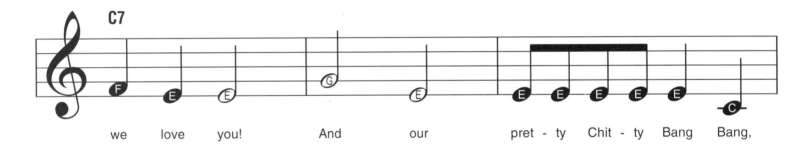

we love you! And our pret-ty Chit-ty Bang Bang,

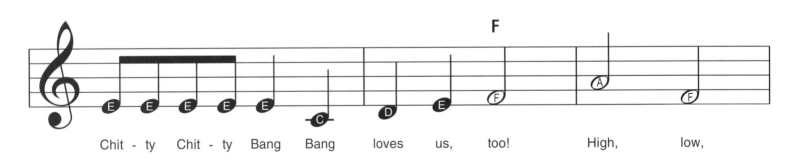

Chit-ty Chit-ty Bang Bang loves us, too! High, low,

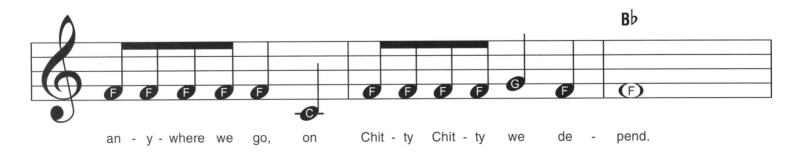

an-y-where we go, on Chit-ty Chit-ty we de-pend.

Consider Yourself
from the Columbia Pictures - Romulus Film OLIVER!

Words and Music by
Lionel Bart

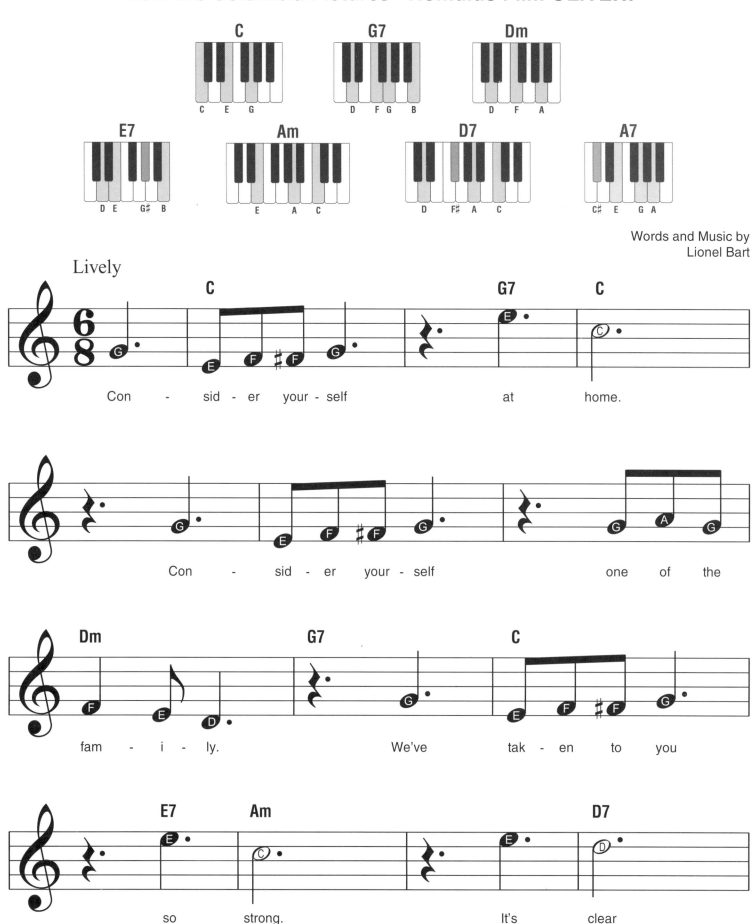

Ding-Dong! The Witch Is Dead

from THE WIZARD OF OZ

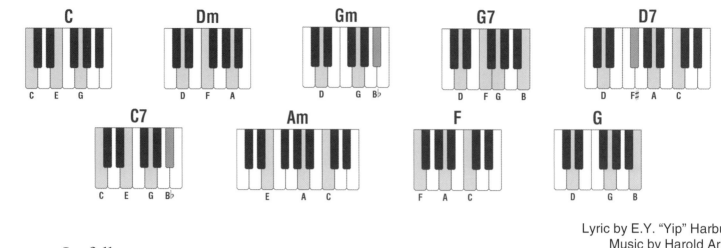

Lyric by E.Y. "Yip" Harburg
Music by Harold Arlen

Joyfully

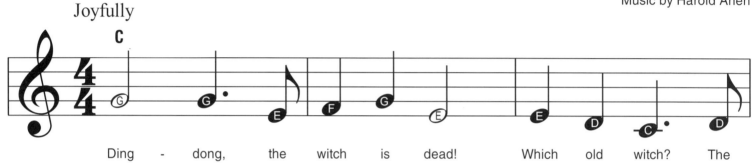

Ding - dong, the witch is dead! Which old witch? The

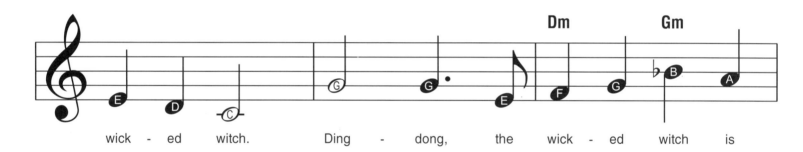

wick - ed witch. Ding - dong, the wick - ed witch is

dead. _____ Wake up, you

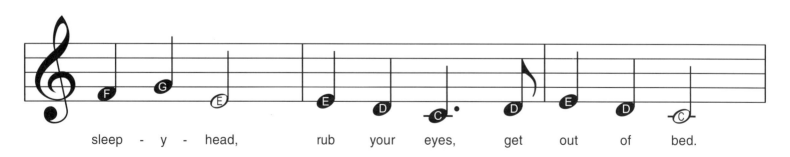

sleep - y - head, rub your eyes, get out of bed.

19

Dites-Moi
(Tell Me Why)
from SOUTH PACIFIC

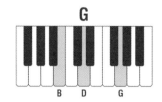

Lyrics by Oscar Hammerstein II
Music by Richard Rodgers

Moderately

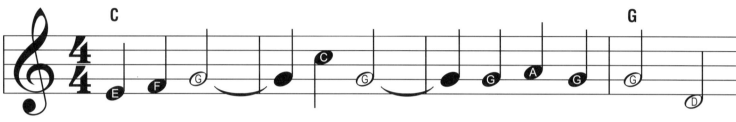

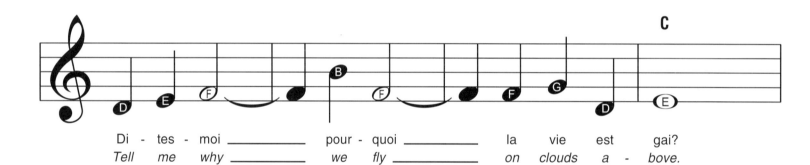

Di - tes - moi _____ pour - quoi _____ la vie est bel - le.
Tell me why _____ the sky _____ is filled with mu - sic.

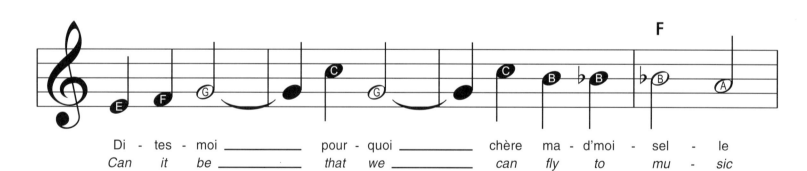

Di - tes - moi _____ pour - quoi _____ la vie est gai?
Tell me why _____ we fly _____ on clouds a - bove.

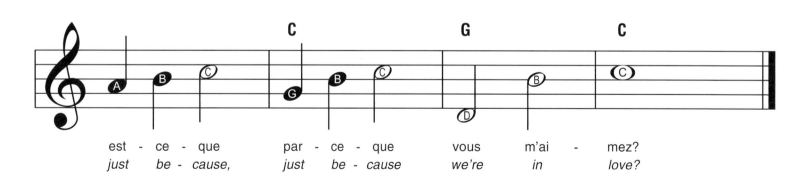

Di - tes - moi _____ pour - quoi _____ chère ma - d'moi - sel - le
Can it be _____ that we _____ can fly to mu - sic

est - ce - que par - ce - que vous m'ai - mez?
just be - cause, just be - cause we're in love?

Happy Birthday to You

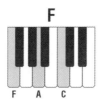
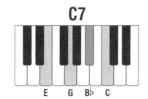
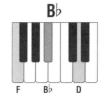

Words and Music by Mildred J. Hill
and Patty S. Hill

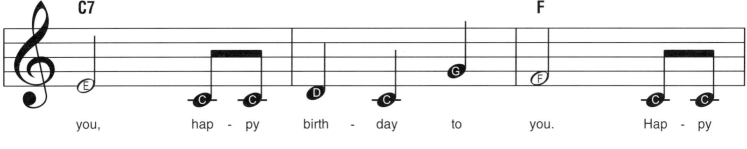

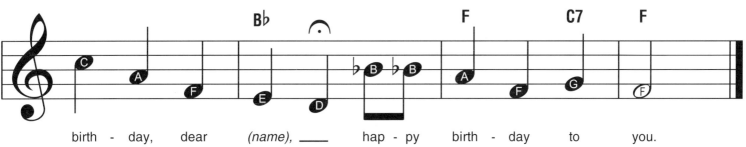

Do-Re-Mi

from THE SOUND OF MUSIC

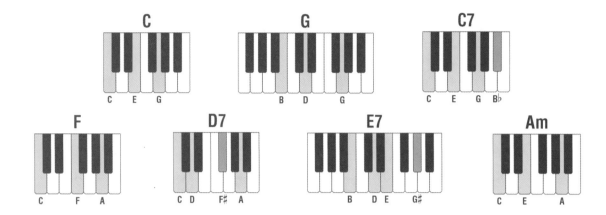

Lyrics by Oscar Hammerstein II
Music by Richard Rodgers

Brightly

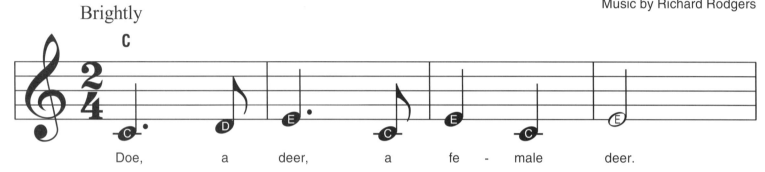

Doe, a deer, a fe - male deer.

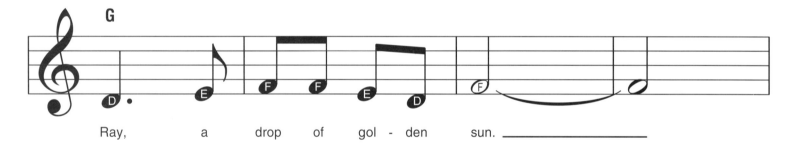

Ray, a drop of gol - den sun. _____

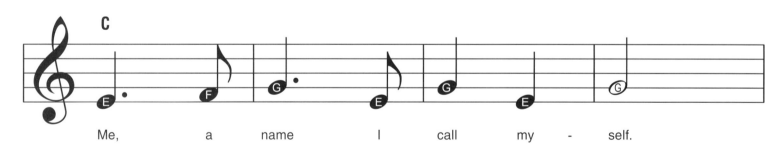

Me, a name I call my - self.

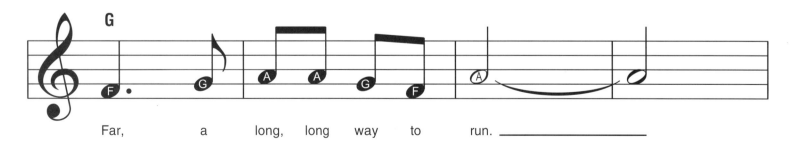

Far, a long, long way to run. _____

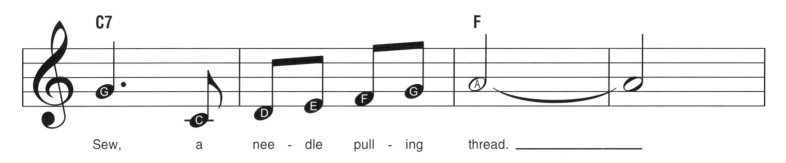

Sew, a nee - dle pull - ing thread. _____

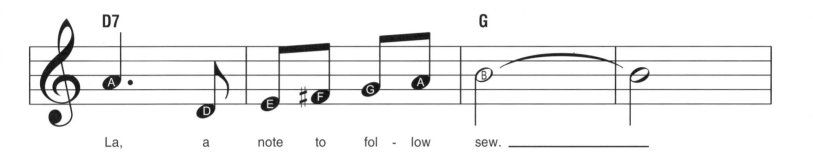

La, a note to fol - low sew. _____

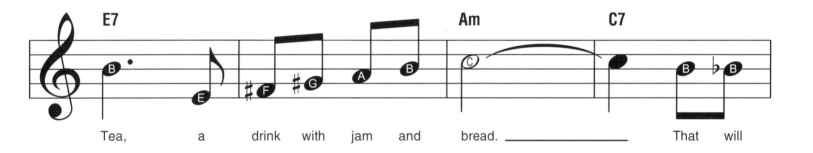

Tea, a drink with jam and bread. _____ That will

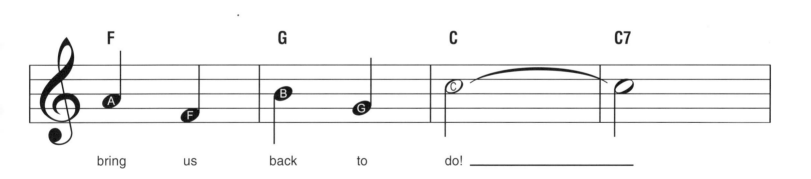

bring us back to do! _____

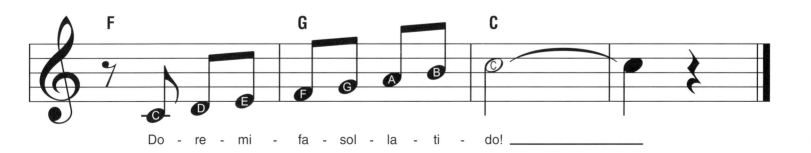

Do - re - mi - fa - sol - la - ti - do! _____

Electricity
from the Broadway Musical BILLY ELLIOT

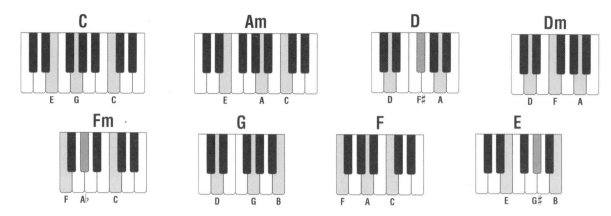

Music by Elton John
Lyrics by Lee Hall

Moderately

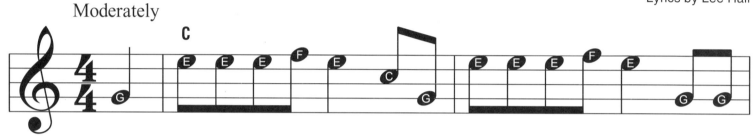

I can't real-ly ex-plain it; I have-n't got the words. It's a

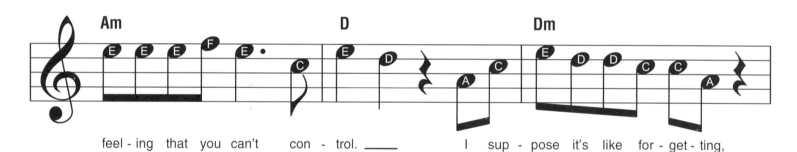

feel-ing that you can't con-trol. ____ I sup-pose it's like for-get-ting,

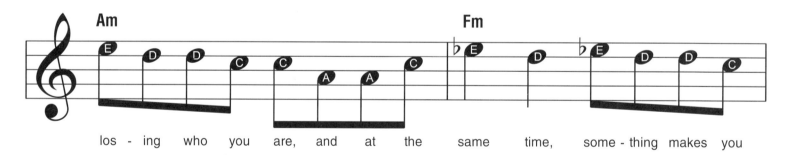

los-ing who you are, and at the same time, some-thing makes you

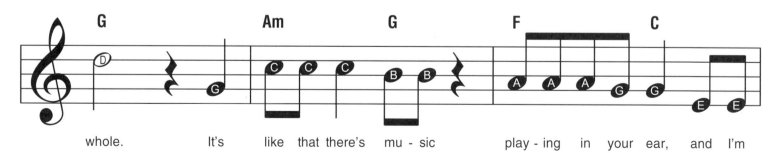

whole. It's like that there's mu-sic play-ing in your ear, and I'm

Getting to Know You
from THE KING AND I

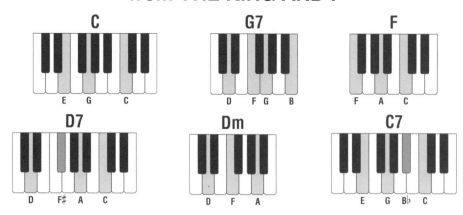

Lyrics by Oscar Hammerstein II
Music by Richard Rodgers

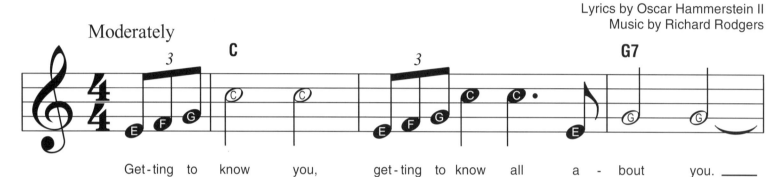

Get-ting to know you, get-ting to know all a-bout you. _____

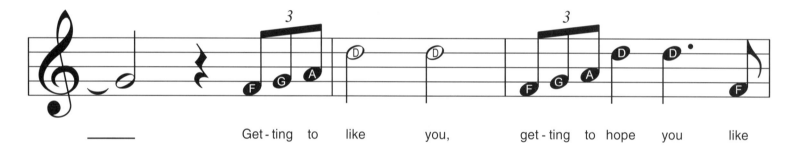

_____ Get-ting to like you, get-ting to hope you like

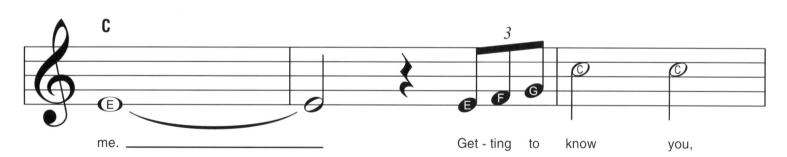

me. _____ Get-ting to know you,

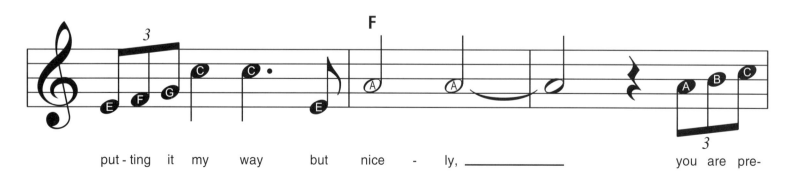

put-ting it my way but nice-ly, _____ you are pre-

Goofus

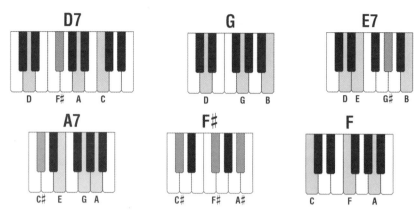

Music by Wayne King and William Harold
Words by Gus Kahn

Bouncy Shuffle

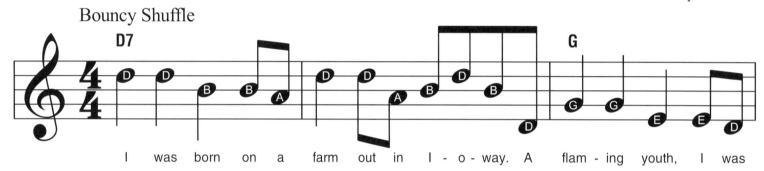

I was born on a farm out in I - o - way. A flam - ing youth, I was

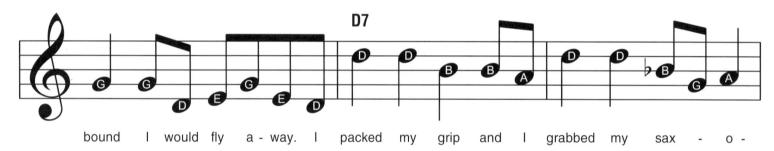

bound I would fly a - way. I packed my grip and I grabbed my sax - o -

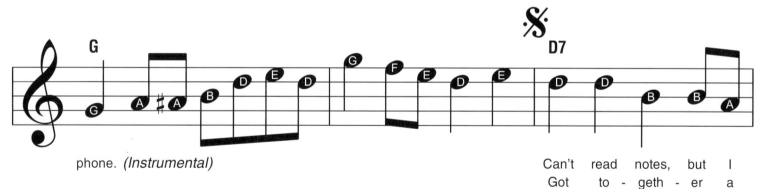

phone. (Instrumental)

Can't read notes, but I
Got to - geth - er a

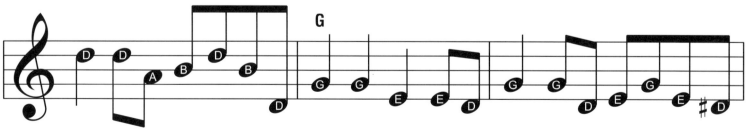

play an - y - thing by ear. I made up tunes on the sounds that I used to hear. When
new kind of or - ches - tree and we all played just the same goof - us har - mo - ny. And

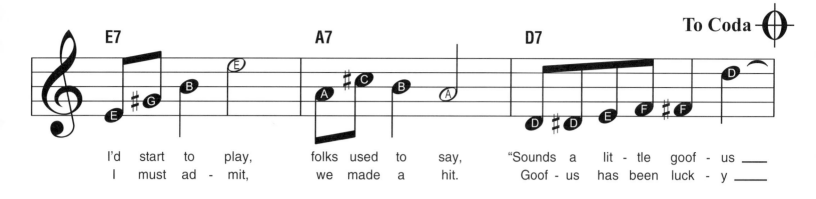

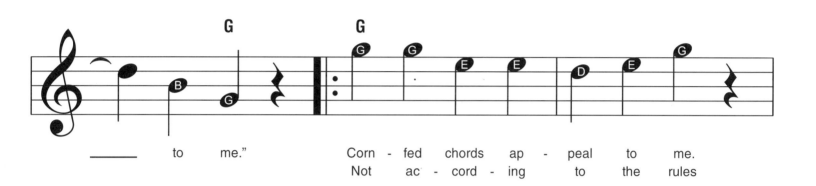

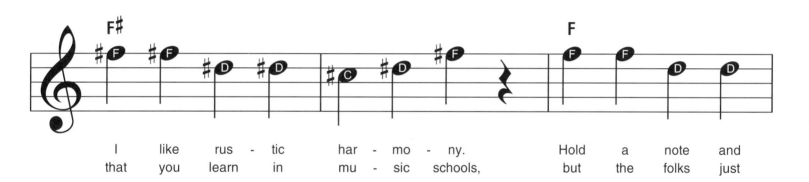

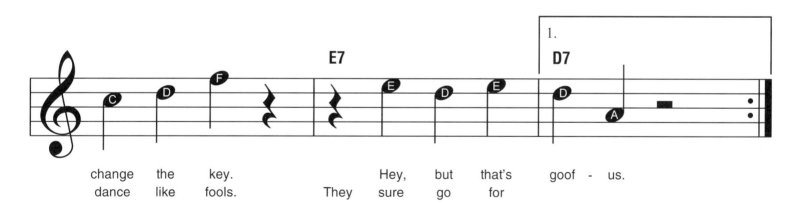

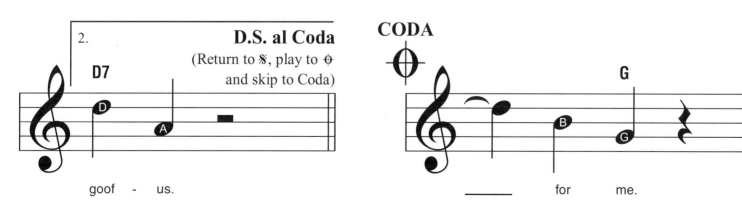

Happy Trails

from the Television Series THE ROY ROGERS SHOW

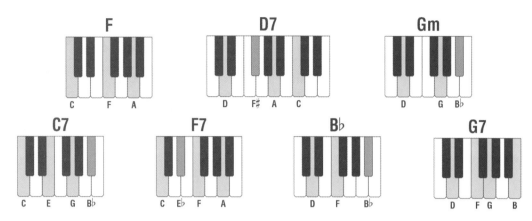

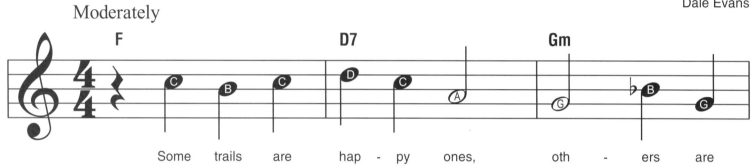

Words and Music by
Dale Evans

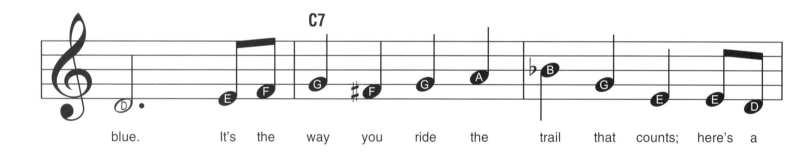

Some trails are hap - py ones, oth - ers are

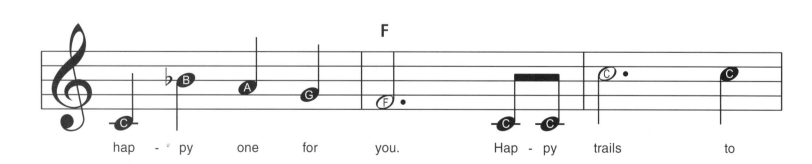

blue. It's the way you ride the trail that counts; here's a

hap - py one for you. Hap - py trails to

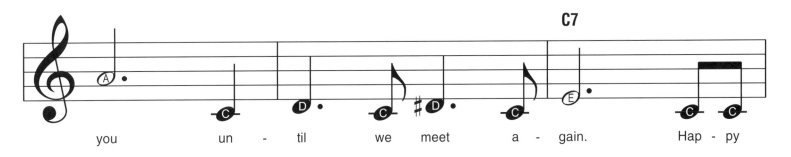

you un - til we meet a - gain. Hap - py

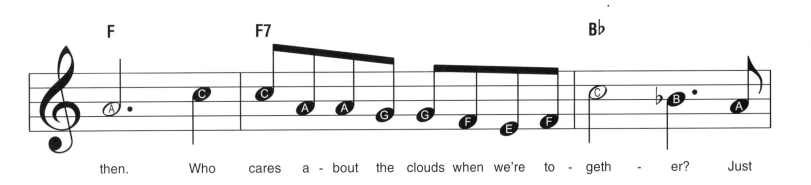

trails to you, keep smil - in' un - til

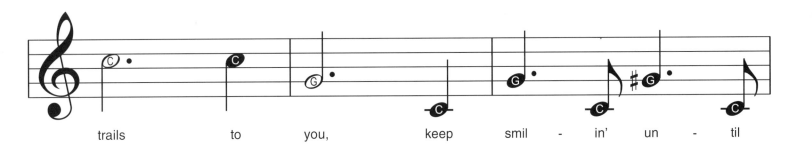

then. Who cares a - bout the clouds when we're to - geth - er? Just

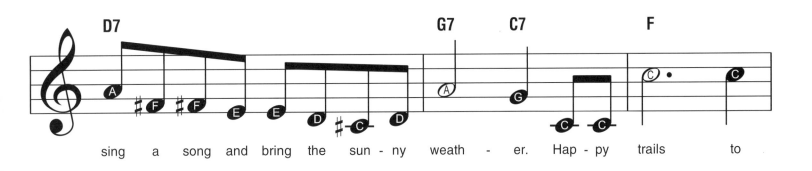

sing a song and bring the sun - ny weath - er. Hap - py trails to

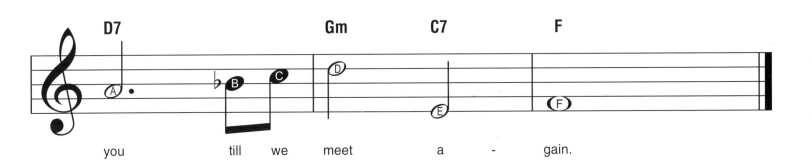

you till we meet a - gain.

He's Got the Whole World in His Hands

 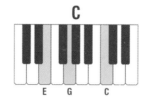

Traditional Spiritual

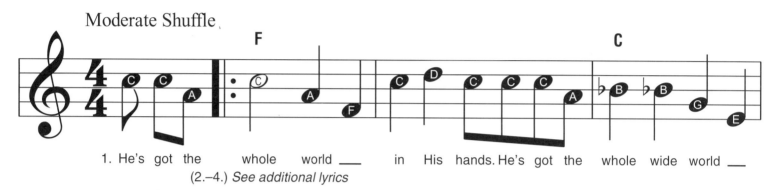

1. He's got the whole world ___ in His hands. He's got the whole wide world ___
(2.–4.) *See additional lyrics*

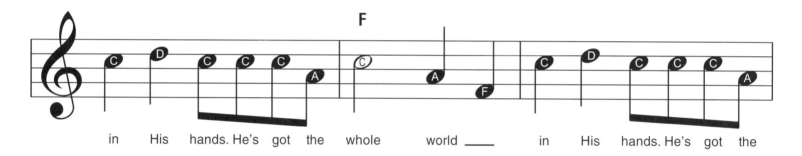

in His hands. He's got the whole world ___ in His hands. He's got the

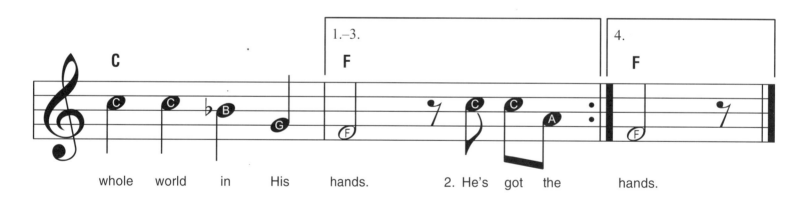

whole world in His hands.   2. He's got the   hands.

Additional Lyrics

2. He's got the wind and the rain in His hands. *(3x)*
   He's got the whole world in His hands.

3. He's got the little tiny baby in His hands. *(3x)*
   He's got the whole world in His hands.

4. He's got everybody here in His hands. *(3x)*
   He's got the whole world in His hands.

The Hokey Pokey

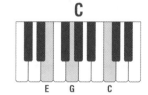

Words and Music by Charles P. Macak,
Tafft Baker and Larry LaPrise

Moderate Shuffle

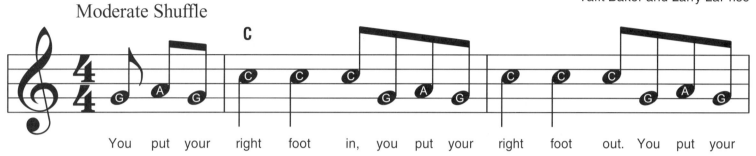

You put your right foot in, you put your right foot out. You put your

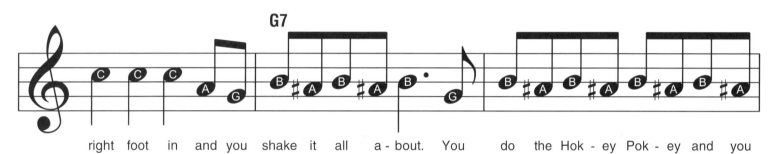

right foot in and you shake it all a - bout. You do the Hok - ey Pok - ey and you

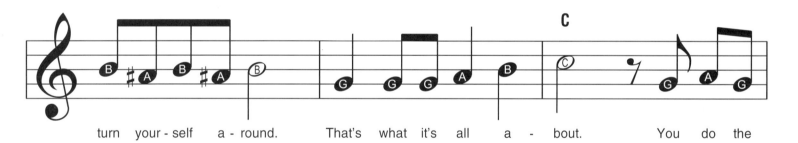

turn your - self a - round. That's what it's all a - bout. You do the

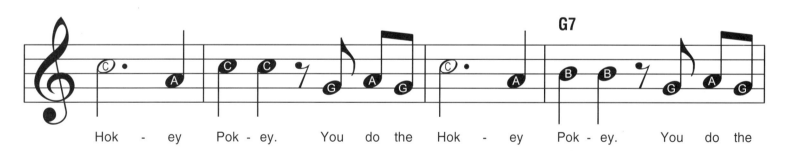

Hok - ey Pok - ey. You do the Hok - ey Pok - ey. You do the

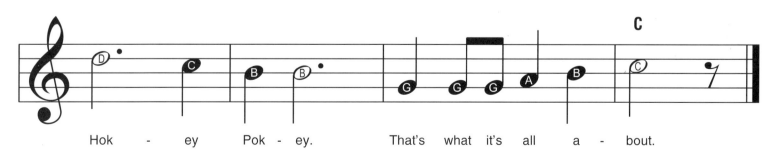

Hok - ey Pok - ey. That's what it's all a - bout.

Heart and Soul
from the Paramount Short Subject A SONG IS BORN

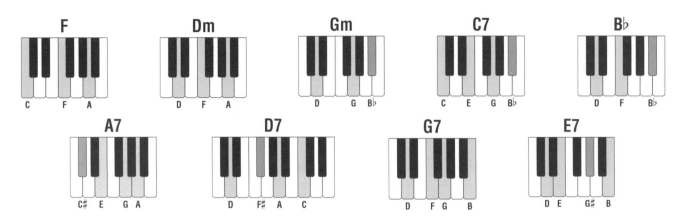

Words by Frank Loesser
Music by Hoagy Carmichael

Moderate Shuffle

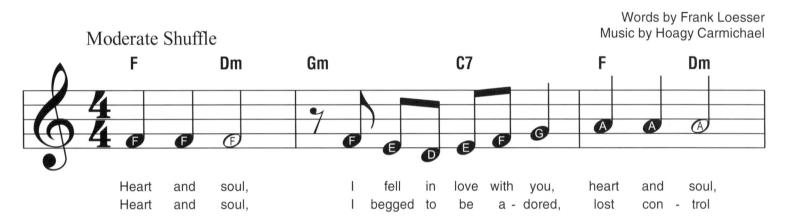

Heart and soul, I fell in love with you, heart and soul,
Heart and soul, I begged to be a - dored, lost con - trol

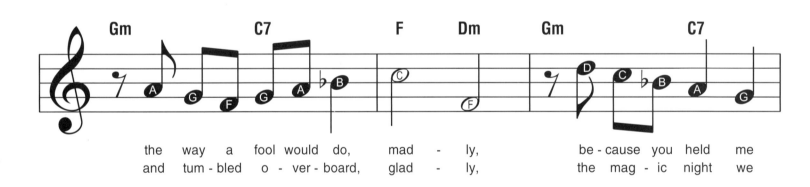

the way a fool would do, mad - ly, be - cause you held me
and tum - bled o - ver - board, glad - ly, the mag - ic night we

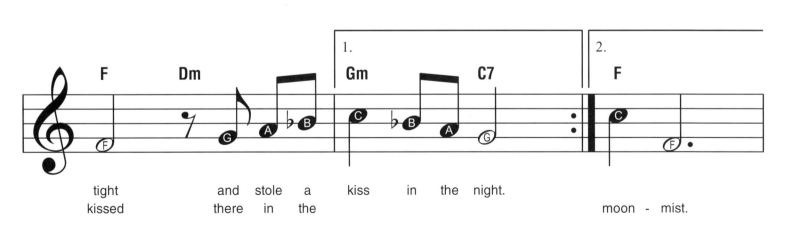

tight and stole a kiss in the night.
kissed there in the moon - mist.

How Much Is That Doggie in the Window

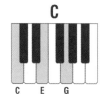

Words and Music by
Bob Merrill

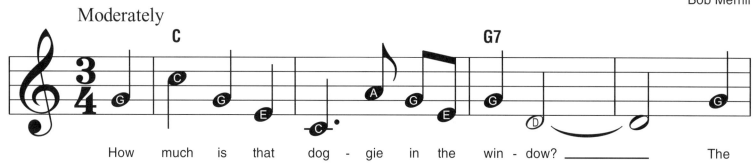

How much is that dog - gie in the win - dow? _____ The

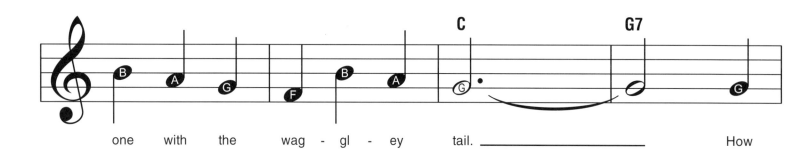

one with the wag - gl - ey tail. _____ How

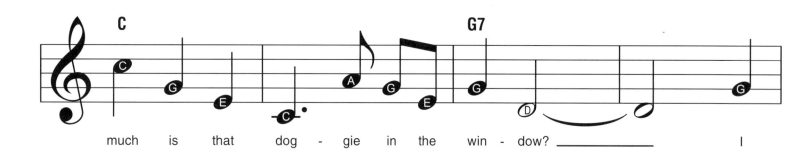

much is that dog - gie in the win - dow? _____ I

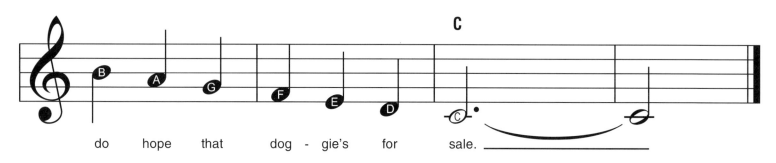

do hope that dog - gie's for sale. _____

Hush, Little Baby

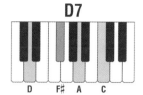

Carolina Folk Lullaby

Moderately

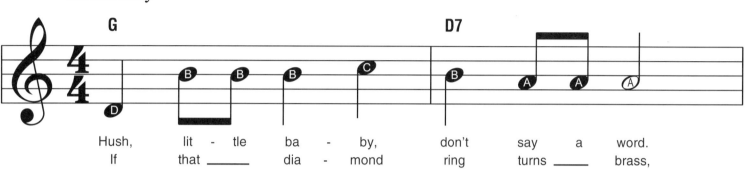

Hush, lit - tle ba - by, don't say a word.
If that _____ dia - mond ring turns _____ brass,

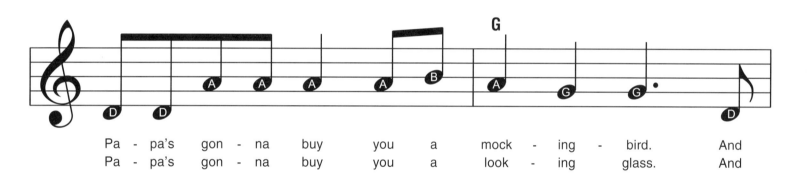

Pa - pa's gon - na buy you a mock - ing - bird. And
Pa - pa's gon - na buy you a look - ing glass. And

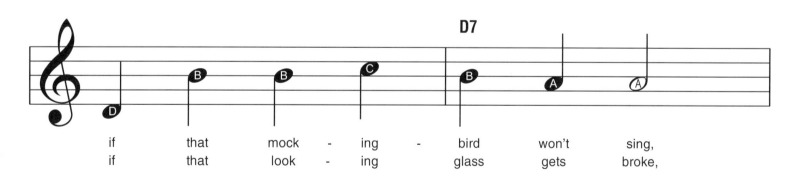

if that mock - ing - bird won't sing,
if that look - ing glass gets broke,

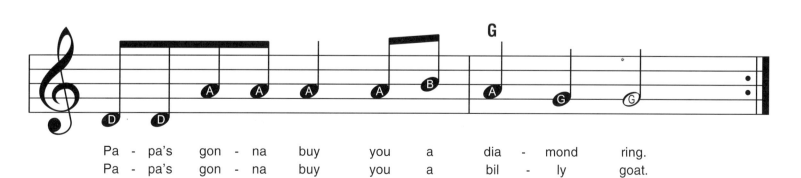

Pa - pa's gon - na buy you a dia - mond ring.
Pa - pa's gon - na buy you a bil - ly goat.

I Whistle a Happy Tune

from THE KING AND I

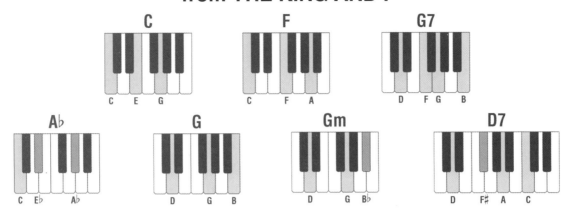

Lyrics by Oscar Hammerstein II
Music by Richard Rodgers

Brightly

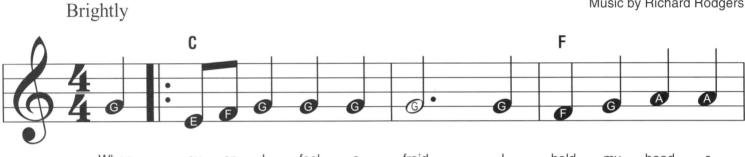

When - ev - er I feel a - fraid, I hold my head e -
shiv - er - ing in my shoes, I strike a care - less

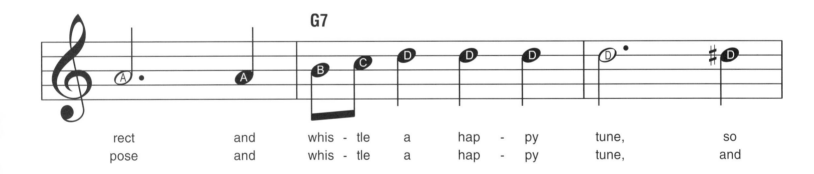

rect and whis - tle a hap - py tune, so
pose and whis - tle a hap - py tune, and

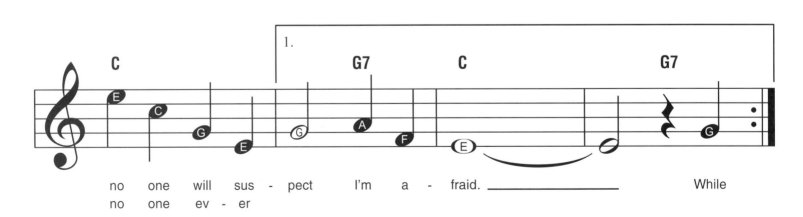

no one will sus - pect I'm a - fraid. _____ While
no one ev - er

I'm an Old Cowhand
(From the Rio Grande)

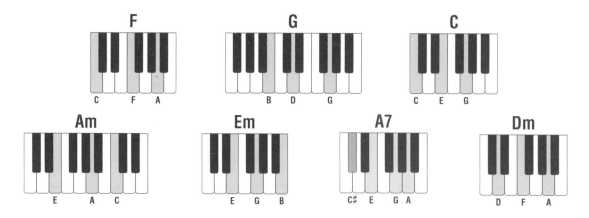

Words and Music by
Johnny Mercer

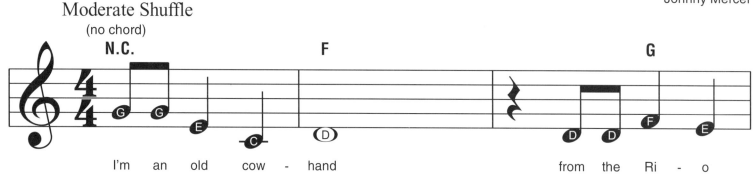

Moderate Shuffle
(no chord)

I'm an old cow - hand   from the Ri - o

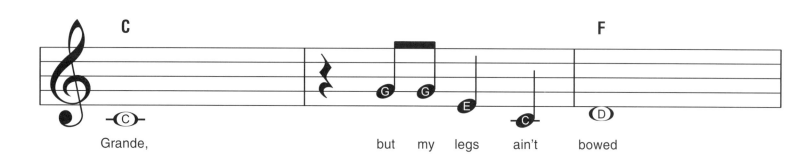

Grande,   but my legs ain't bowed

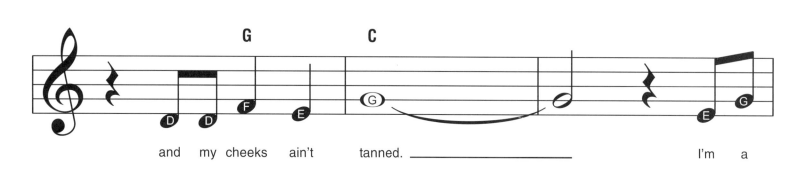

and my cheeks ain't   tanned. _____   I'm a

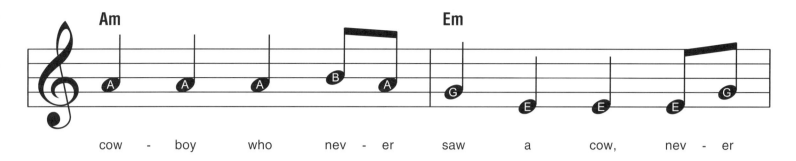

cow - boy who nev - er saw a cow, nev - er

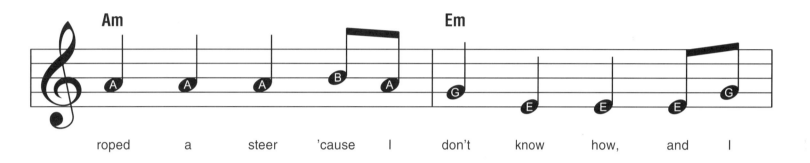

roped a steer 'cause I don't know how, and I

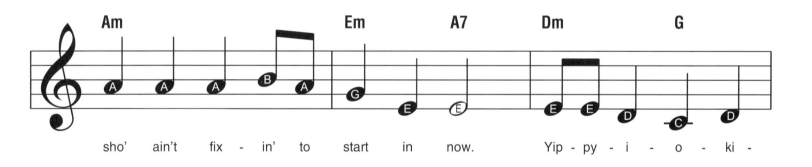

sho' ain't fix - in' to start in now. Yip - py - i - o - ki -

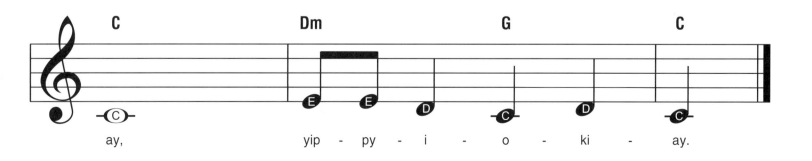

ay, yip - py - i - o - ki - ay.

I'm Popeye the Sailor Man
Theme from the Paramount Cartoon POPEYE THE SAILOR

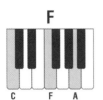 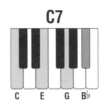 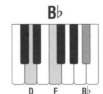 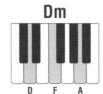

Words and Music by
Sammy Lerner

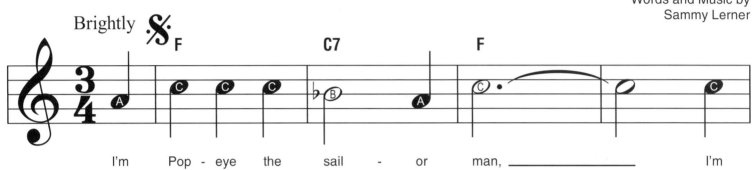

I'm Pop - eye the sail - or man, _____ I'm

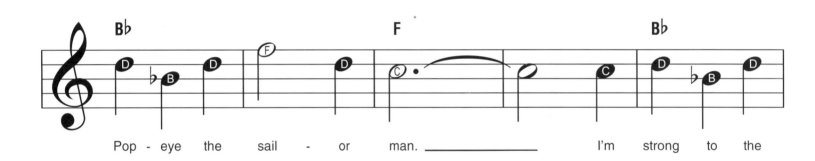

Pop - eye the sail - or man. _____ I'm strong to the

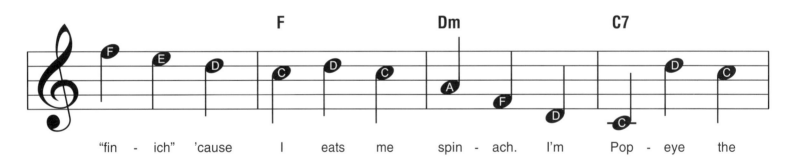

"fin - ich" 'cause I eats me spin - ach. I'm Pop - eye the

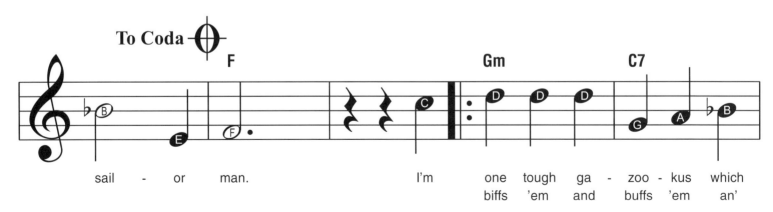

sail - or man.   I'm one tough ga - zoo - kus which

biffs 'em and buffs 'em an'

I've Been Working on the Railroad

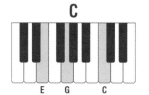
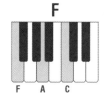

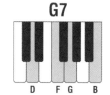
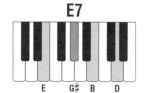

American Folksong

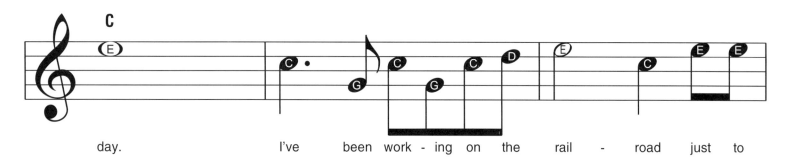
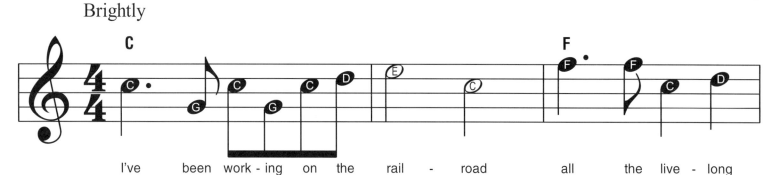
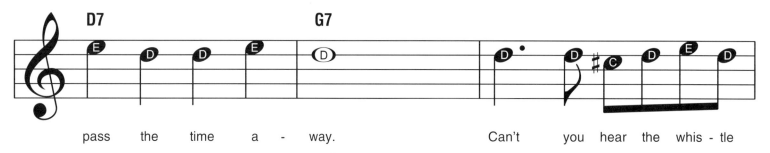
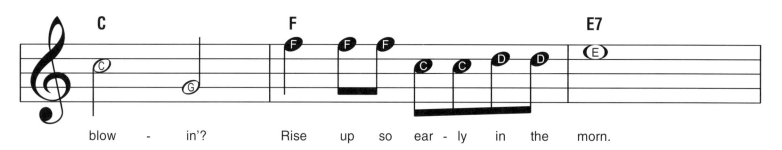
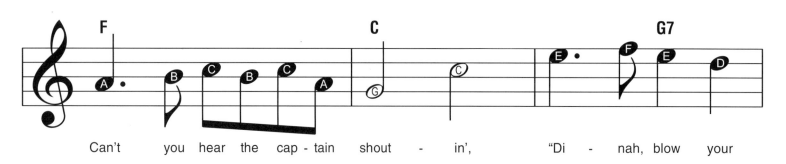

If I Only Had a Brain

from THE WIZARD OF OZ

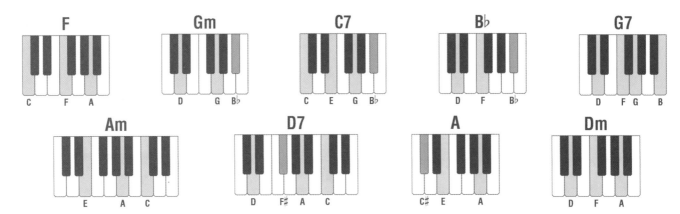

Lyric by E.Y. "Yip" Harburg
Music by Harold Arlen

I could while a-way the ho-urs, con-fer-rin' with the flow-ers, con-
rav-el ev-'ry rid-dle for an-y in-di-vid-le in

sult-in' with the rain. _____ And my head I'd be scratch-in' while my
trou-ble or in pain. _____ With the thoughts I'd be think-in', I could

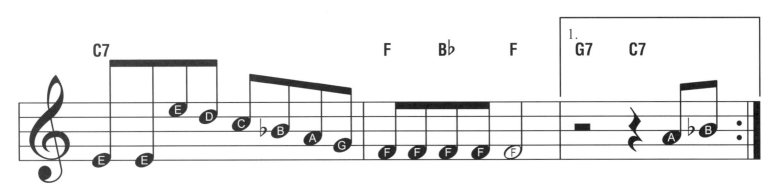

thoughts were bus-y hatch-in' if I on-ly had a brain. I'd un-
be an-oth-er Lin-coln if I on-ly had a brain.

It's a Small World

from Disneyland Resort® and Magic Kingdom® Park

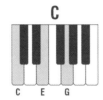  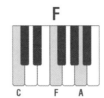 

Words and Music by Richard M. Sherman
and Robert B. Sherman

Brightly

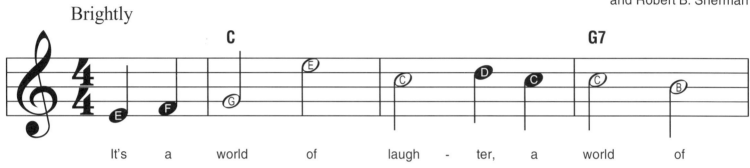

It's a world of laugh - ter, a world of

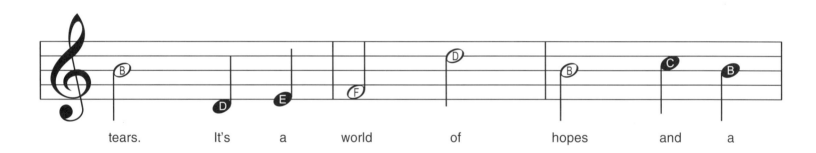

tears. It's a world of hopes and a

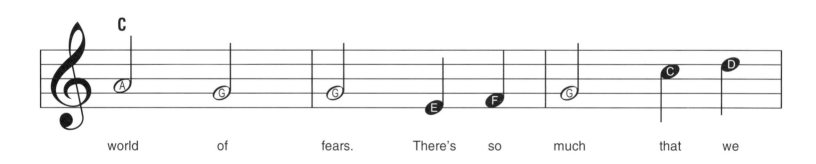

world of fears. There's so much that we

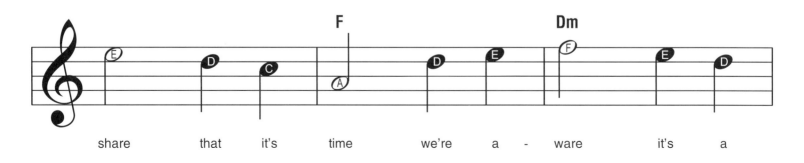

share that it's time we're a - ware it's a

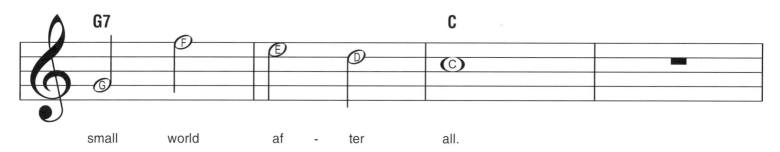

small world af - ter all.

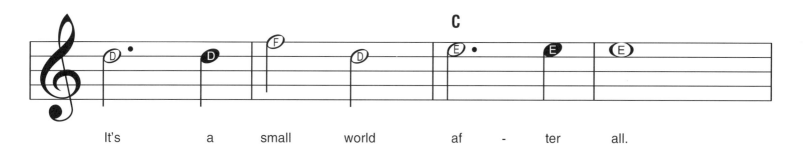

It's a small world af - ter all.

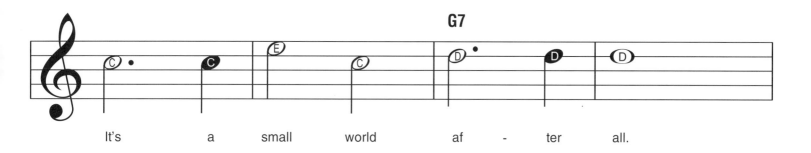

It's a small world af - ter all.

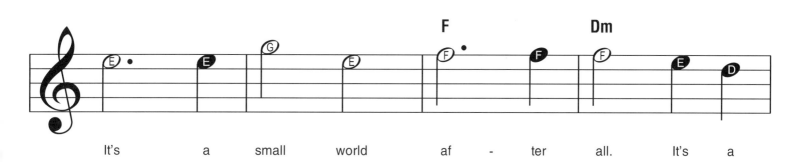

It's a small world af - ter all. It's a

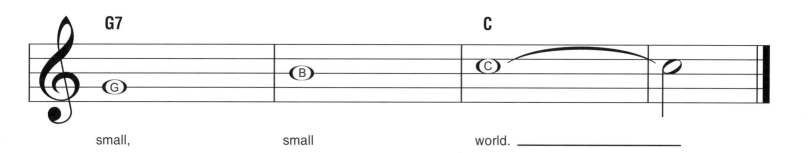

small, small world. _____

It's the Hard-Knock Life

from the Musical Production ANNIE

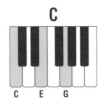
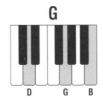
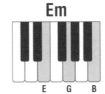
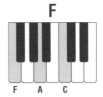

Lyric by Martin Charnin
Music by Charles Strouse

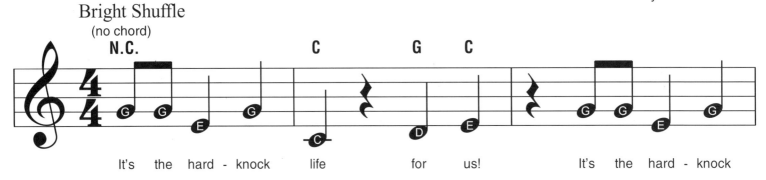

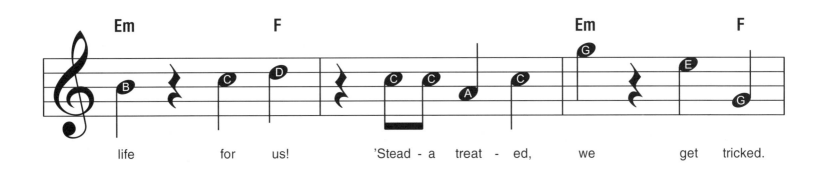

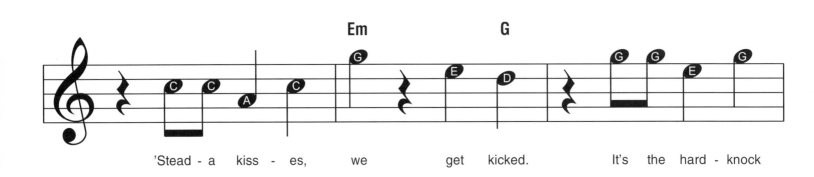

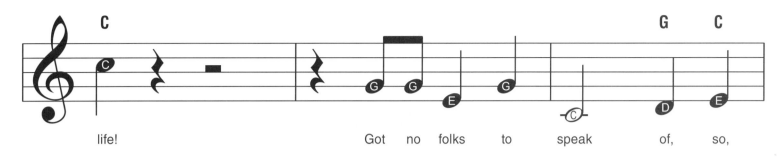

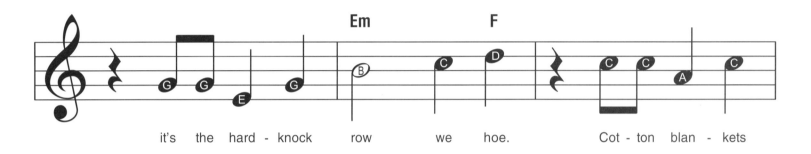

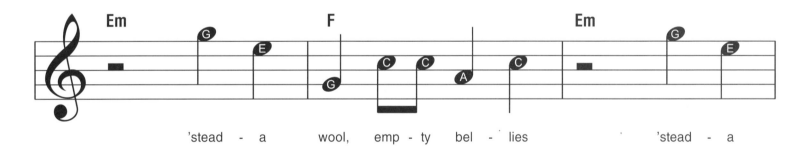

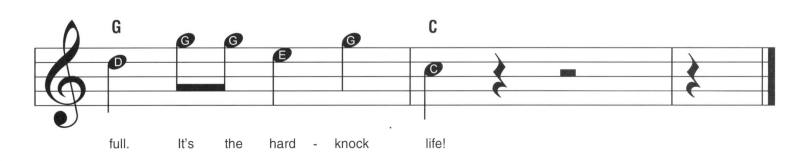

John Jacob Jingleheimer Schmidt

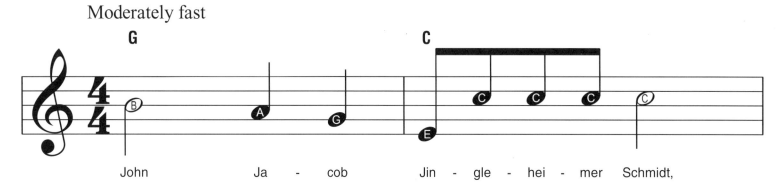

Traditional

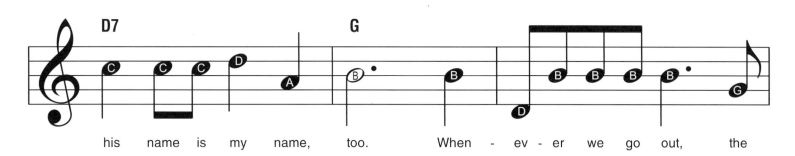

John Ja - cob Jin - gle - hei - mer Schmidt,

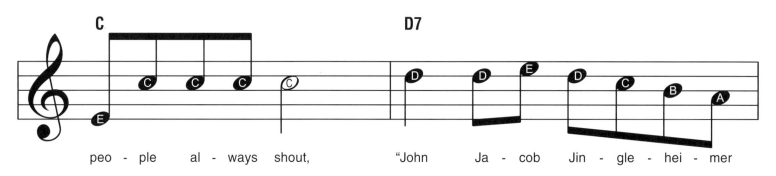

his name is my name, too. When - ev - er we go out, the

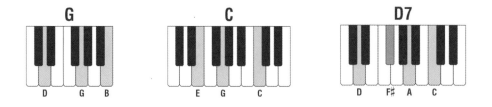

peo - ple al - ways shout, "John Ja - cob Jin - gle - hei - mer

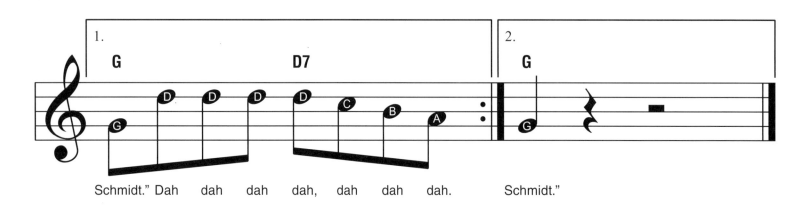

Schmidt." Dah dah dah dah, dah dah dah.   Schmidt."

Kumbaya

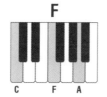
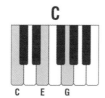

Congo Folksong

Kum - ba - ya, my Lord, _____ kum - ba - ya.

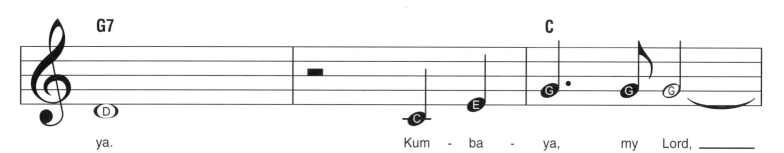

Kum - ba - ya, my Lord, _____ kum - ba -

ya.   Kum - ba - ya, my Lord, _____

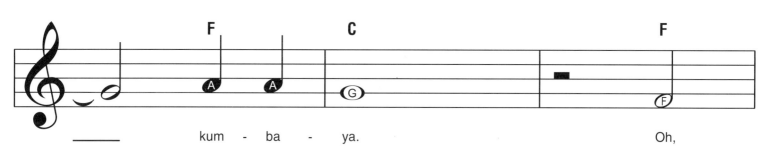

_____ kum - ba - ya.   Oh,

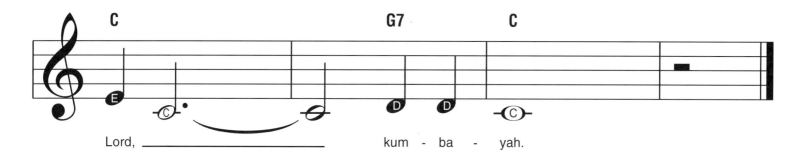

Lord, _____ kum - ba - yah.

Let Me Entertain You

from GYPSY

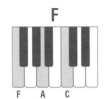
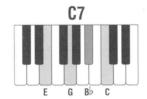
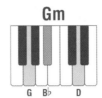
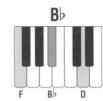
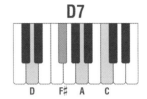

Lyrics by Stephen Sondheim
Music by Jule Styne

Moderately

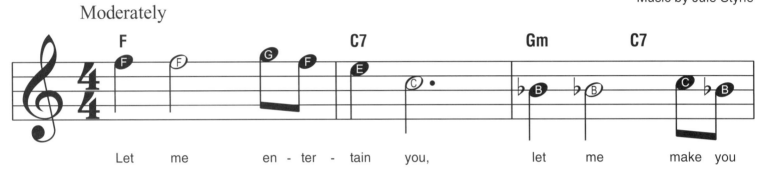

Let me en - ter - tain you, let me make you

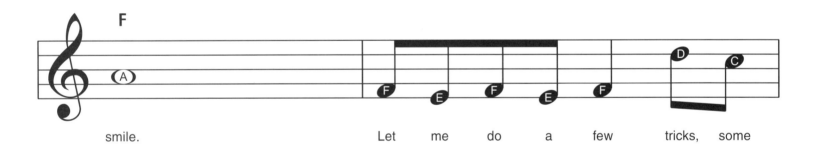

smile. Let me do a few tricks, some

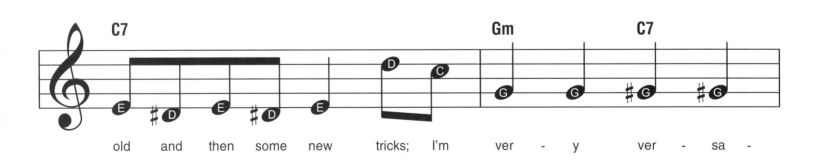

old and then some new tricks; I'm ver - y ver - sa -

tile.   And if you're real good, I'll make you feel good.

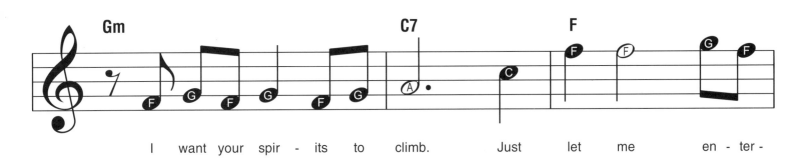

I want your spir - its to climb. Just let me en - ter -

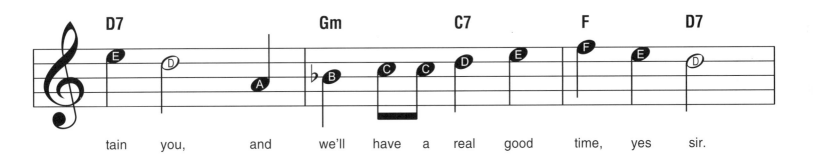

tain you, and we'll have a real good time, yes sir.

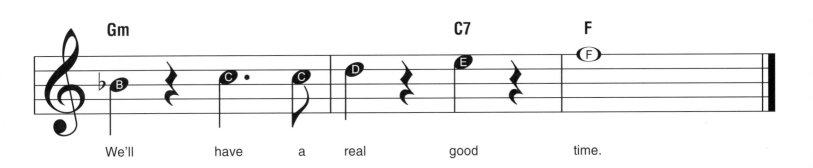

We'll have a real good time.

Little People
from LES MISÉRABLES

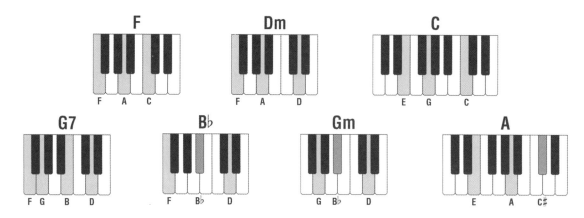

Music by Claude-Michel Schönberg
Lyrics by Alain Boublil,
Jean-Marc Natel and Herbert Kretzmer

Moderate Shuffle

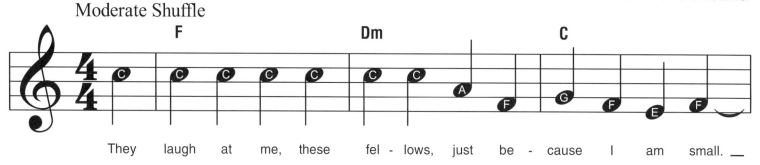

They laugh at me, these fel - lows, just be - cause I am small. __

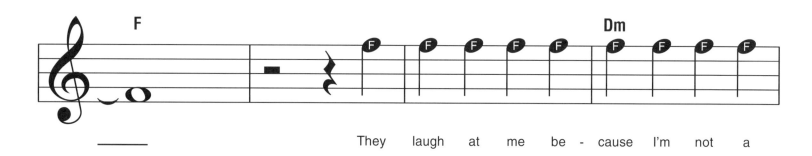

__ They laugh at me be - cause I'm not a

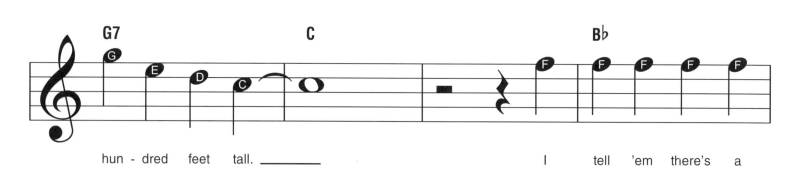

hun - dred feet tall. _____ I tell 'em there's a

Maybe
from the Musical Production ANNIE

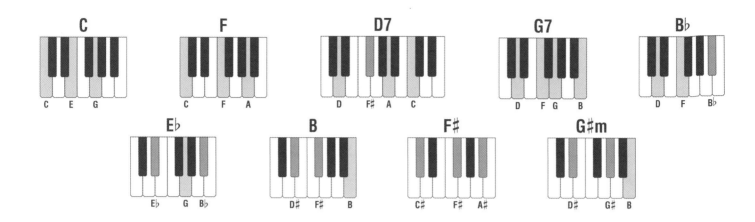

Lyric by Martin Charnin
Music by Charles Strouse

Moderately

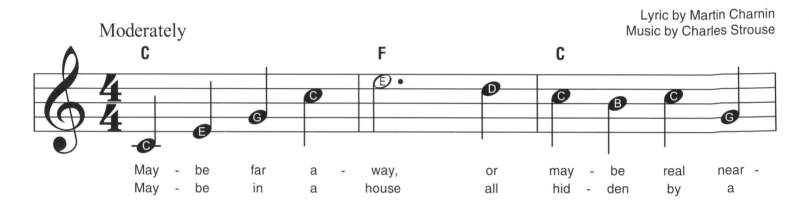

May - be far a - way, or may - be real near -
May - be in a house all hid - den by a

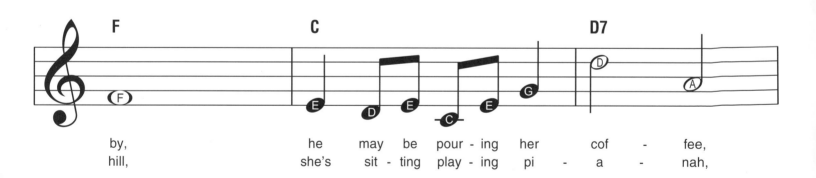

by, he may be pour - ing her cof - fee,
hill, she's sit - ting play - ing pi - a - nah,

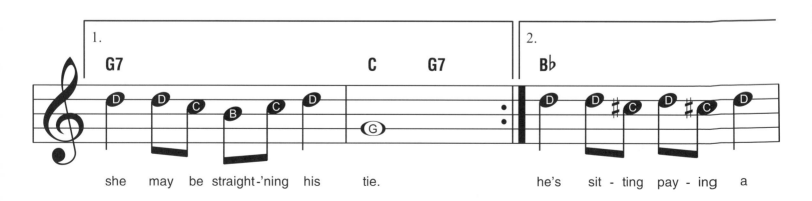

she may be straight -'ning his tie.
he's sit - ting pay - ing a

Mickey Mouse March

from Walt Disney's THE MICKEY MOUSE CLUB

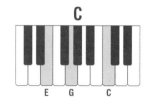
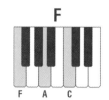
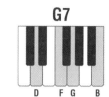
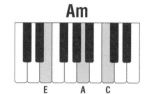
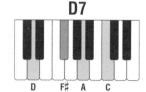

Words and Music by
Jimmie Dodd

Bright March

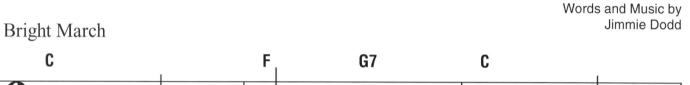

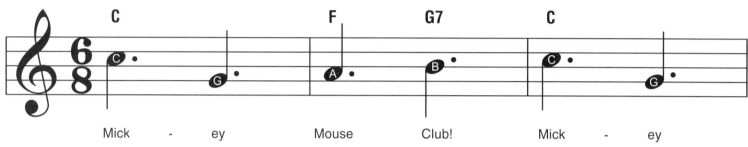

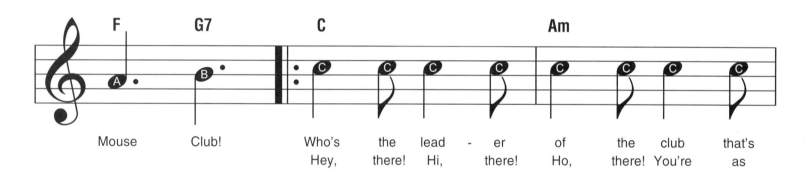

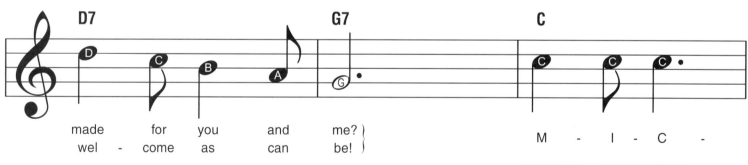

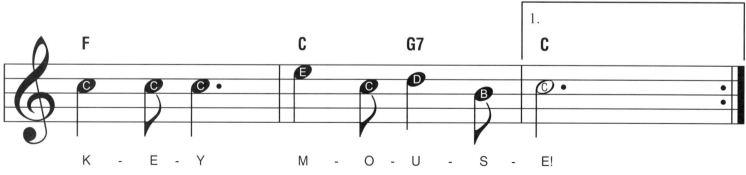

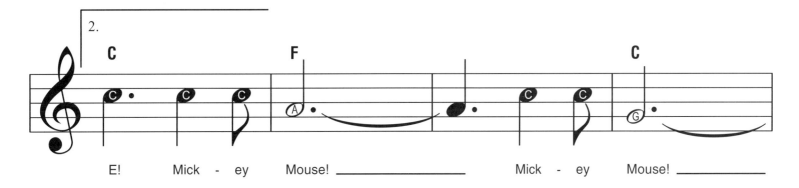

E! Mick - ey Mouse! _____ Mick - ey Mouse! _____

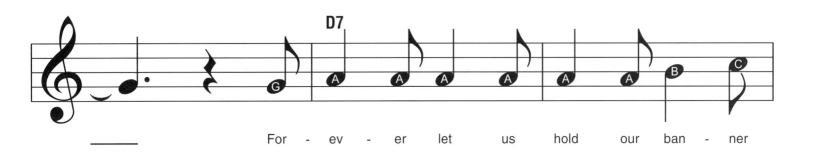

_____ For - ev - er let us hold our ban - ner high!

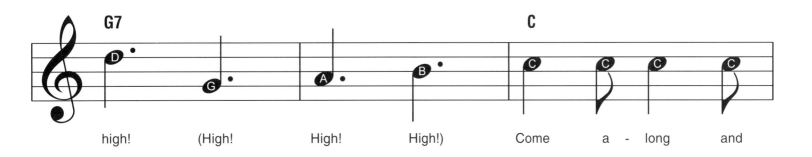

(High! High! High!) Come a - long and

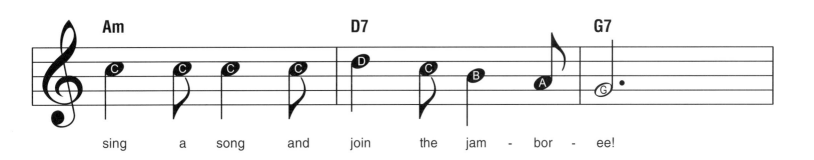

sing a song and join the jam - bor - ee!

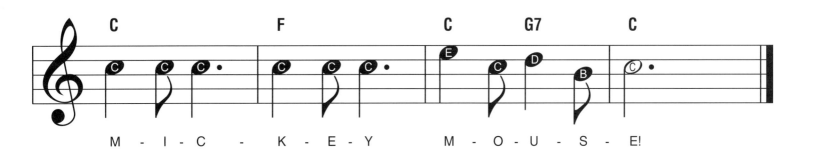

M - I - C - K - E - Y M - O - U - S - E!

My Favorite Things
from THE SOUND OF MUSIC

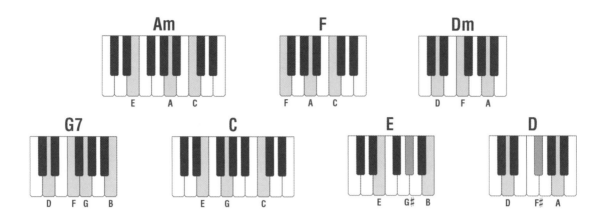

Lyrics by Oscar Hammerstein II
Music by Richard Rodgers

Moderately

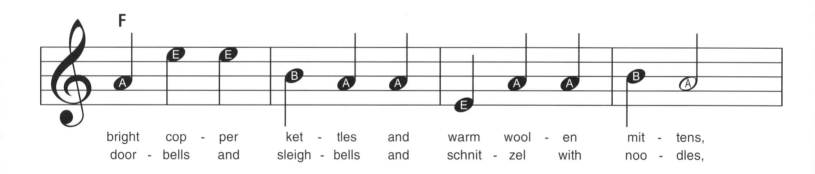

Rain - drops on ros - es and whis - kers on kit - tens,
Cream - col - ored po - nies and crisp ap - ple stru - dels,

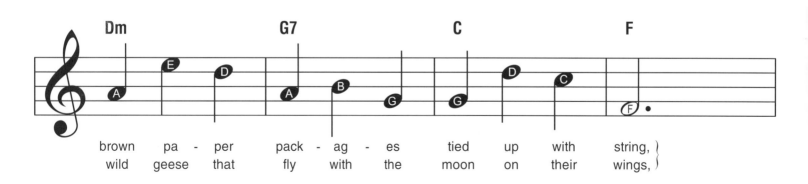

bright cop - per ket - tles and warm wool - en mit - tens,
door - bells and sleigh - bells and schnit - zel with noo - dles,

brown pa - per pack - ag - es tied up with string,
wild geese that fly with the moon on their wings,

Naughty
from MATILDA THE MUSICAL

Words and Music by
Tim Minchin

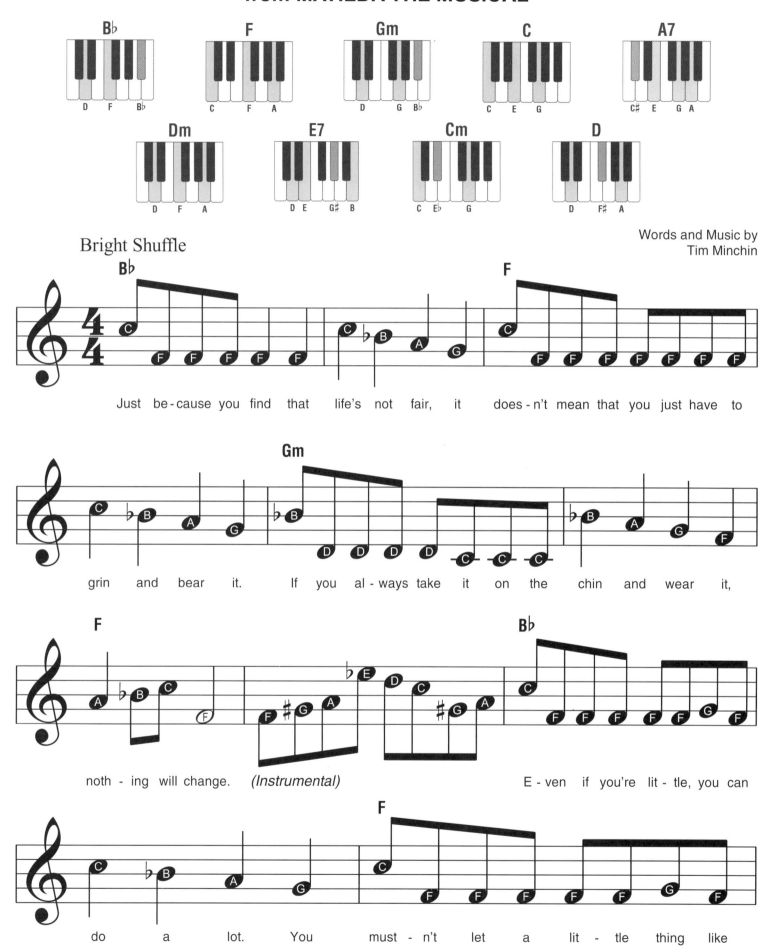

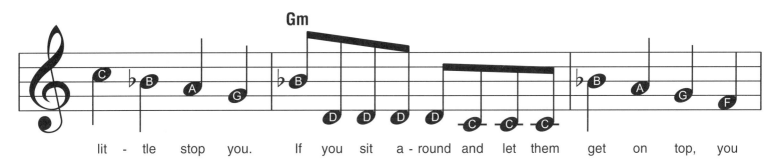

lit - tle stop you. If you sit a - round and let them get on top, you

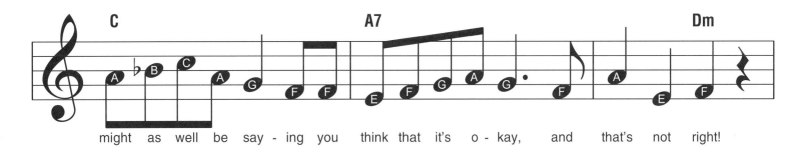

might as well be say - ing you think that it's o - kay, and that's not right!

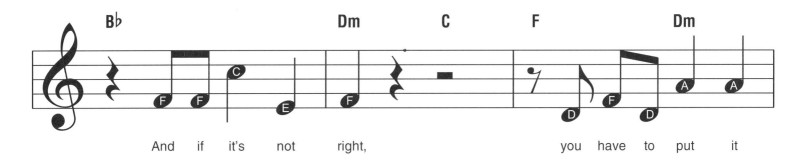

And if it's not right, you have to put it

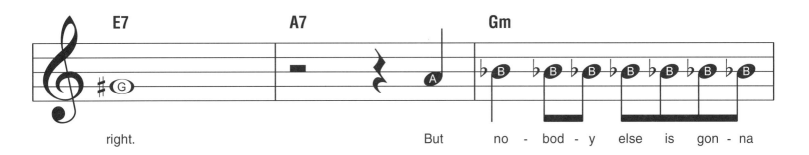

right. But no - bod - y else is gon - na

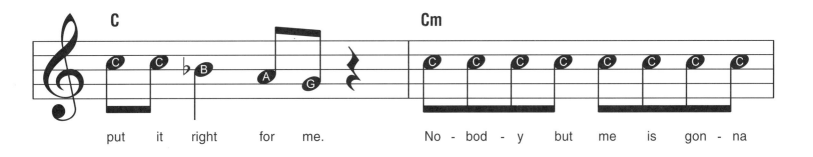

put it right for me. No - bod - y but me is gon - na

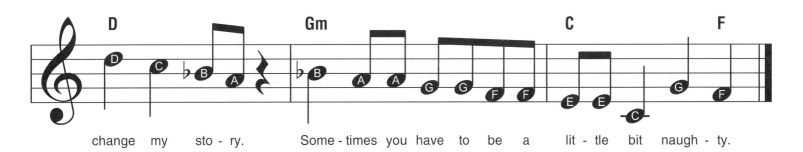

change my sto - ry. Some - times you have to be a lit - tle bit naugh - ty.

On Top of Spaghetti

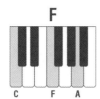
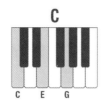
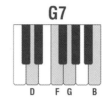

Words and Music by
Tom Glazer

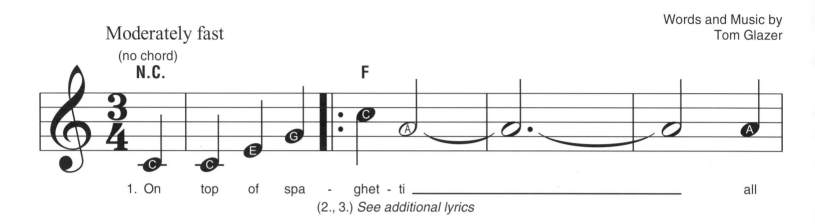

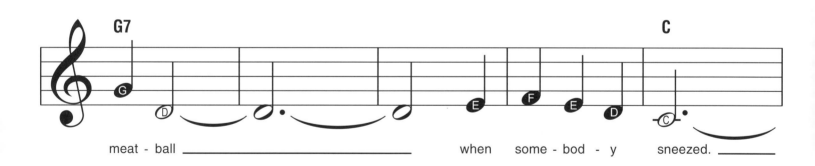

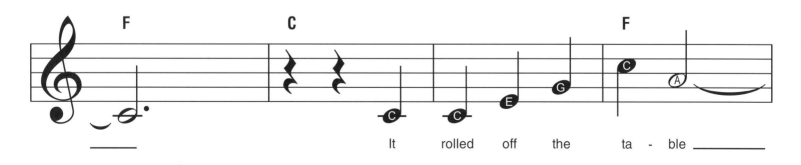

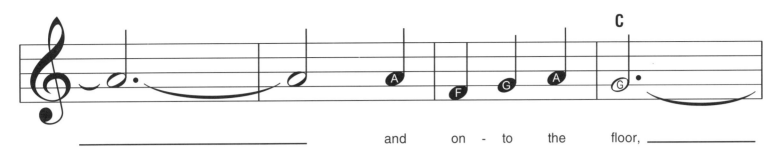

and on - to the floor, _____

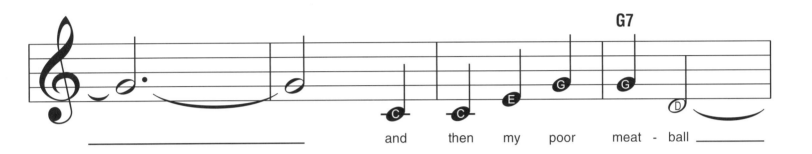

and then my poor meat - ball _____

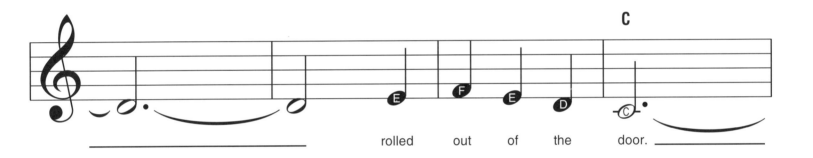

rolled out of the door. _____

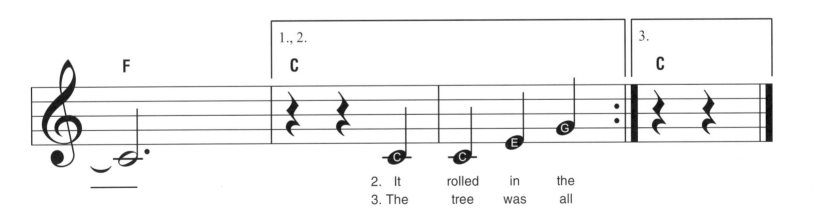

2. It rolled in the
3. The tree was all

Additional Lyrics

2. It rolled in the garden and under a bush,
   And then my poor meatball was nothing but mush.
   The mush was as tasty as tasty could be,
   And early next summer, it grew into a tree.

3. The tree was all covered with beautiful moss;
   It grew lovely meatballs and tomato sauce.
   So if you eat spaghetti all covered with cheese,
   Hold on to your meatballs and don't ever sneeze!

Over the Rainbow

from THE WIZARD OF OZ

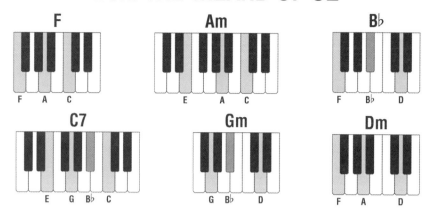

Music by Harold Arlen
Lyric by E.Y. "Yip" Harburg

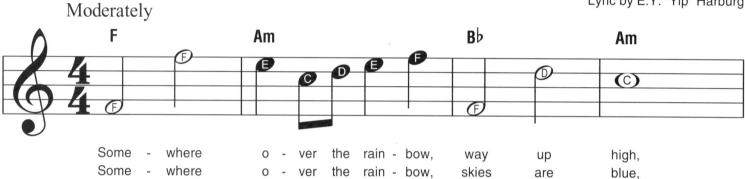

Some - where   o - ver the rain - bow,   way   up   high,
Some - where   o - ver the rain - bow,   skies   are   blue,

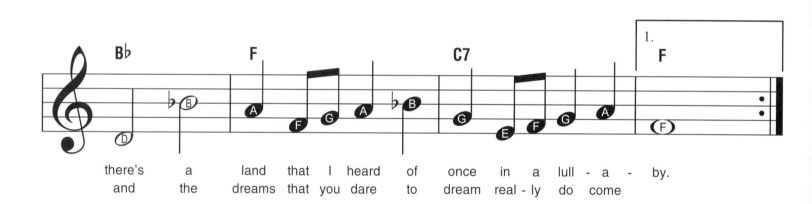

there's   a   land   that I   heard   of   once   in a   lull - a - by.
and   the   dreams   that you   dare   to   dream   real - ly   do   come

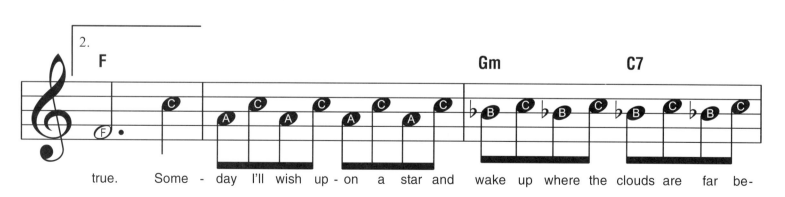

true.   Some - day   I'll   wish   up - on   a   star   and   wake   up   where the   clouds   are   far   be-

Over the River and Through the Woods

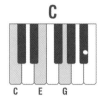
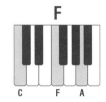
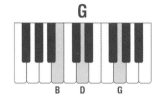

Traditional

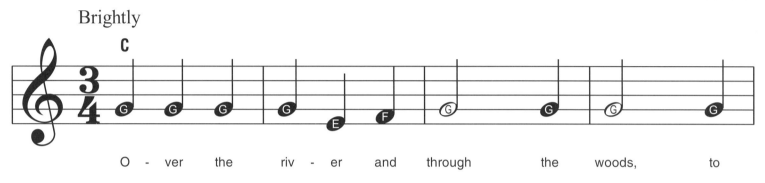

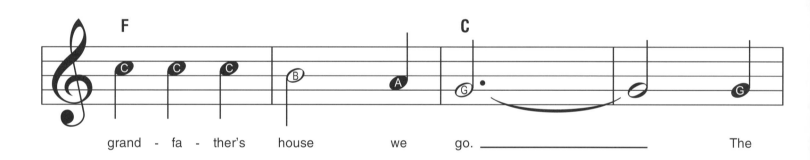

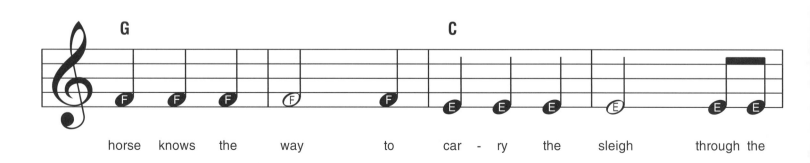

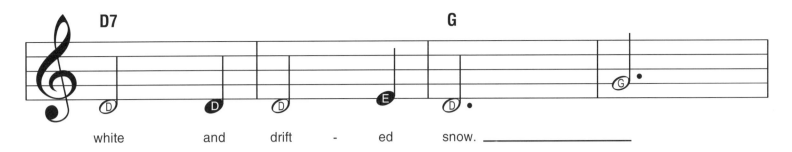

white · and · drift · - · ed · snow. _____

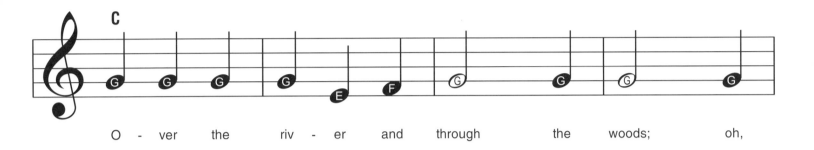

O · - · ver · the · riv · - · er · and · through · the · woods; · oh,

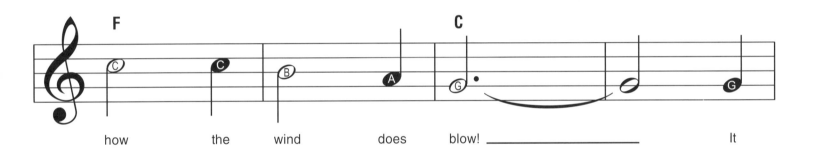

how · the · wind · does · blow! _____ · It

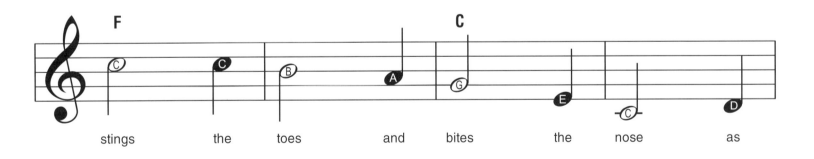

stings · the · toes · and · bites · the · nose · as

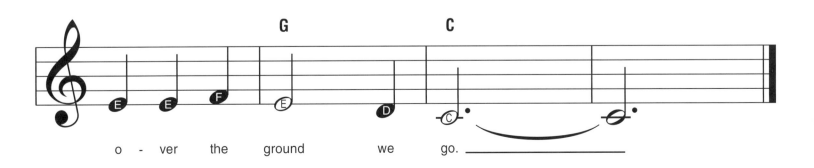

o · - · ver · the · ground · we · go. _____

Peter Cottontail

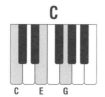
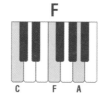
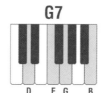
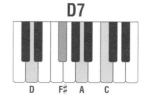

Words and Music by Steve Nelson
and Jack Rollins

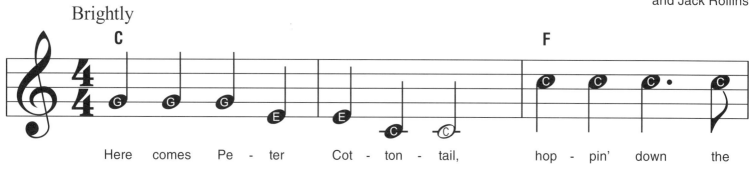

Here comes Pe - ter Cot - ton - tail, hop - pin' down the

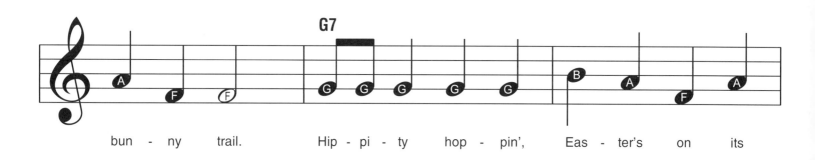

bun - ny trail. Hip - pi - ty hop - pin', Eas - ter's on its

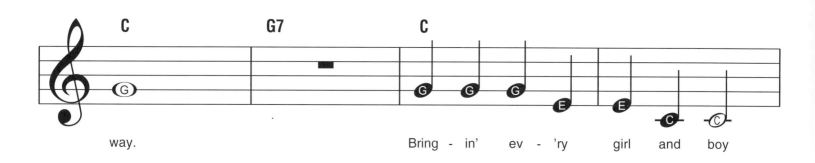

way. Bring - in' ev - 'ry girl and boy

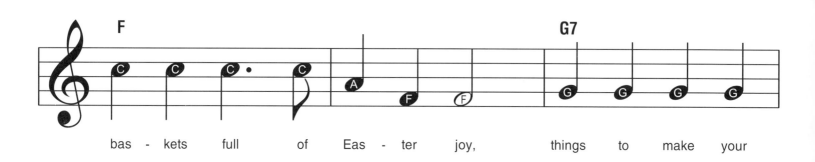

bas - kets full of Eas - ter joy, things to make your

Puff the Magic Dragon

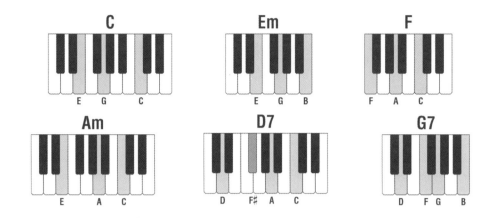

Words and Music by Lenny Lipton
and Peter Yarrow

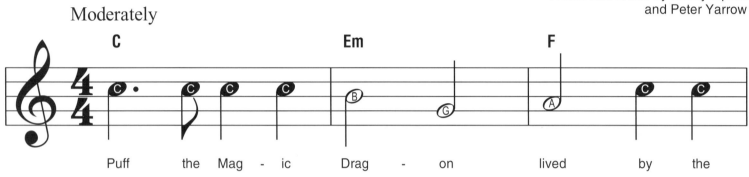

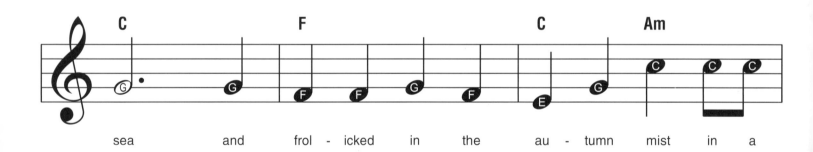

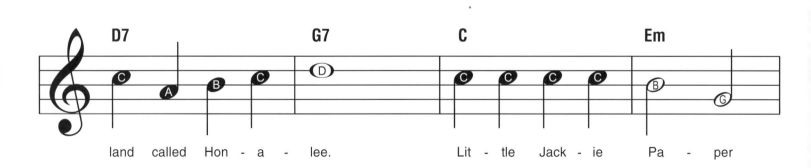

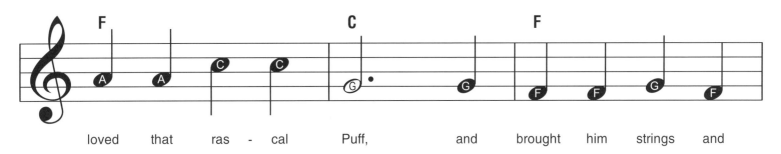

loved that ras - cal Puff, and brought him strings and

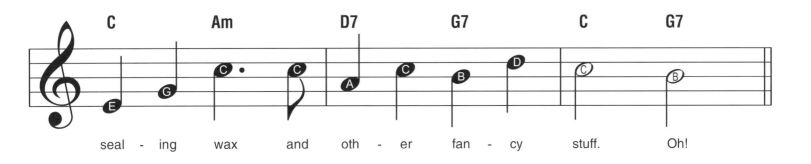

seal - ing wax and oth - er fan - cy stuff. Oh!

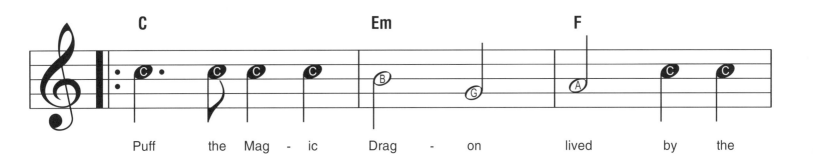

Puff the Mag - ic Drag - on lived by the

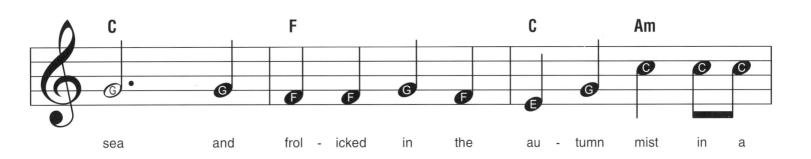

sea and frol - icked in the au - tumn mist in a

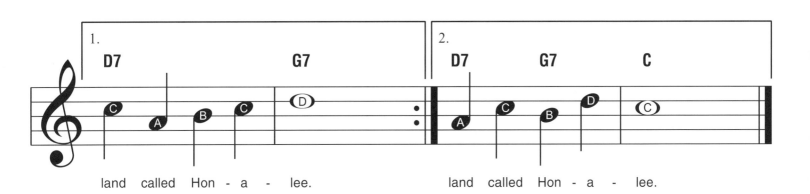

land called Hon - a - lee.   land called Hon - a - lee.

The Rainbow Connection
from THE MUPPET MOVIE

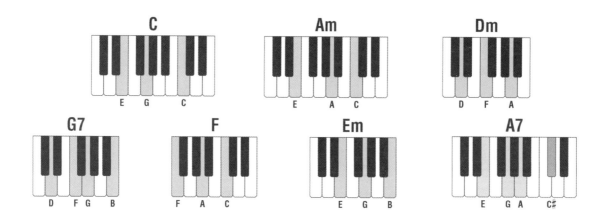

Words and Music by Paul Williams
and Kenneth L. Ascher

Moderately

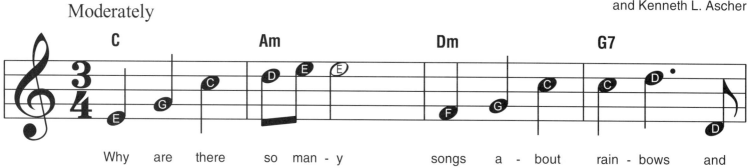

Why are there so man-y songs a-bout rain-bows and

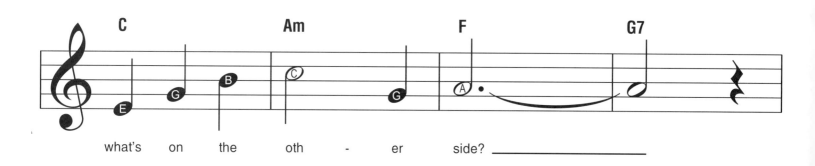

what's on the oth-er side? _____

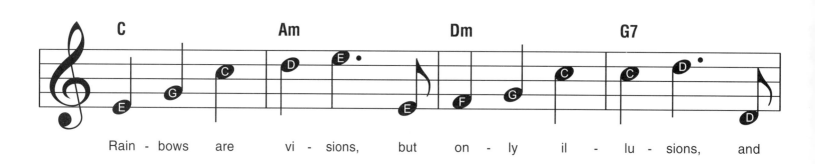

Rain-bows are vi-sions, but on-ly il-lu-sions, and

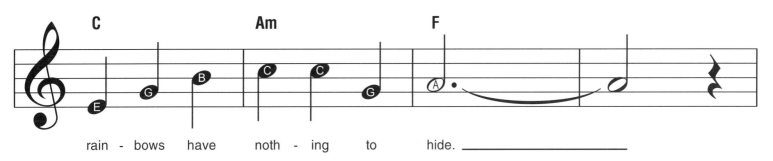

rain - bows have noth - ing to hide. _____

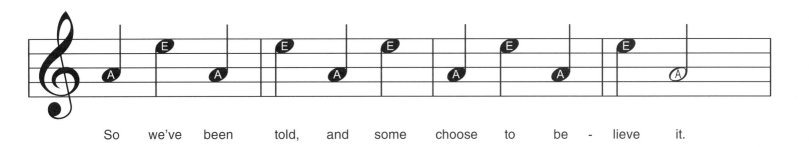

So we've been told, and some choose to be - lieve it.

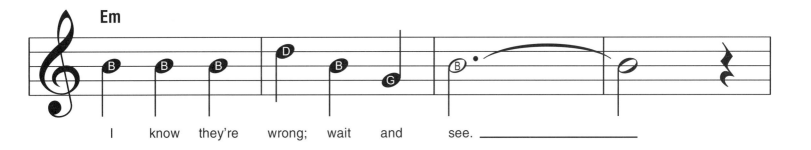

I know they're wrong; wait and see. _____

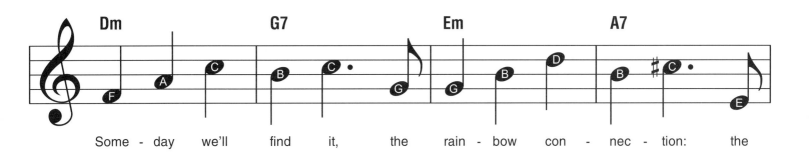

Some - day we'll find it, the rain - bow con - nec - tion: the

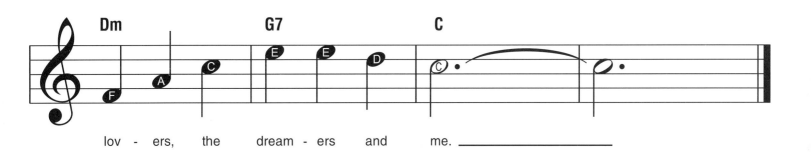

lov - ers, the dream - ers and me. _____

Rubber Duckie
from the Television Series SESAME STREET

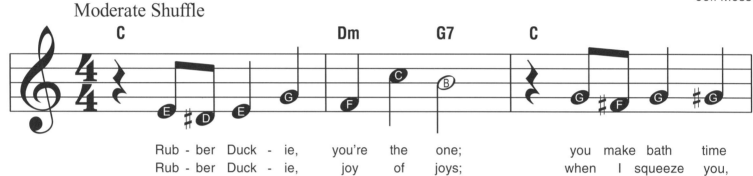

Words and Music by
Jeff Moss

Moderate Shuffle

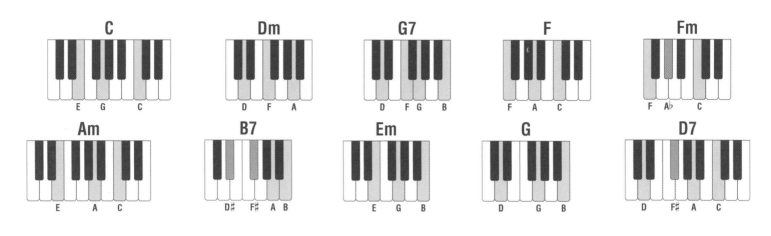

Rub - ber Duck - ie, you're the one; you make bath time
Rub - ber Duck - ie, joy of joys; when I squeeze you,

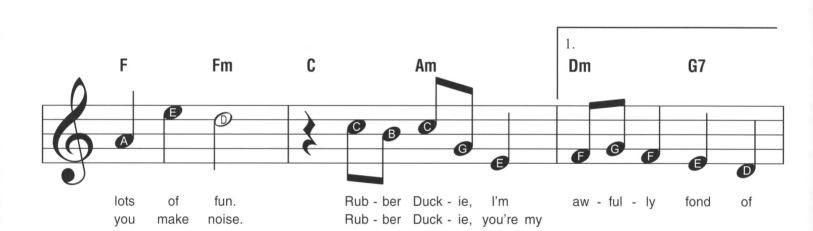

lots of fun. Rub - ber Duck - ie, I'm aw - ful - ly fond of
you make noise. Rub - ber Duck - ie, you're my

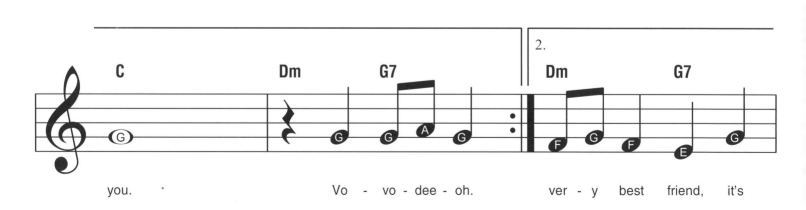

you. Vo - vo - dee - oh. ver - y best friend, it's

Sesame Street Theme
from the Television Series SESAME STREET

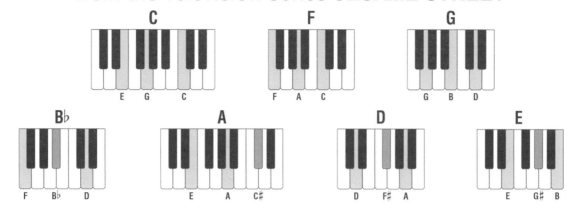

Words by Bruce Hart,
Jon Stone and Joe Raposo
Music by Joe Raposo

Moderate Shuffle

1., 3. Sun - ny day, sweep - in' the clouds a -
2. Come and play! Ev - 'ry - thing's A - O -

way. On my way to where the
K. Friend - ly neigh - bors there, that's

air is sweet. _____
where we meet. _____

Can you tell me how to

get, how to get to Ses - a - me Street? *(Instrumental)*

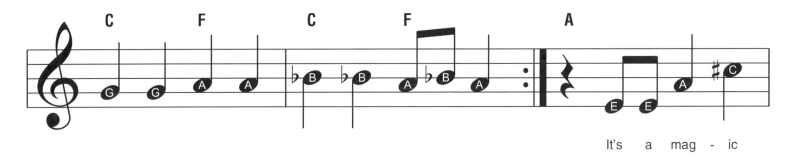

It's a mag - ic

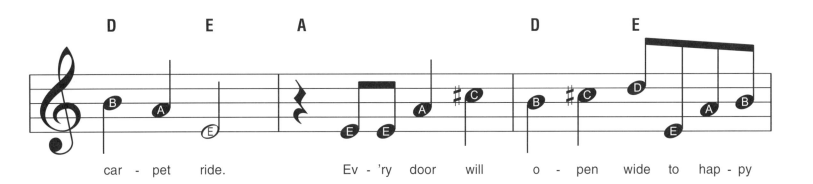

car - pet ride. Ev - 'ry door will o - pen wide to hap - py

D.C. al Coda
(Return to beginning,
play to ⊕ and skip to Coda)

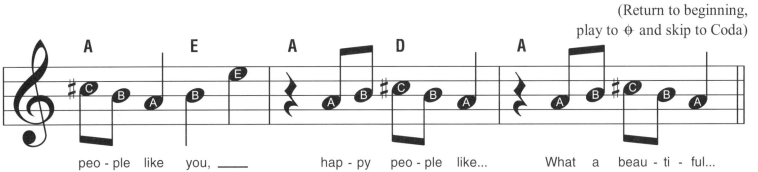

peo - ple like you, _____ hap - py peo - ple like... What a beau - ti - ful...

CODA

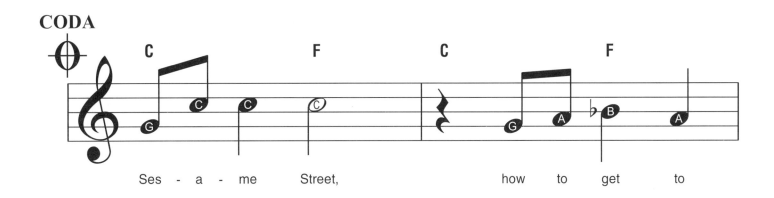

Ses - a - me Street, how to get to

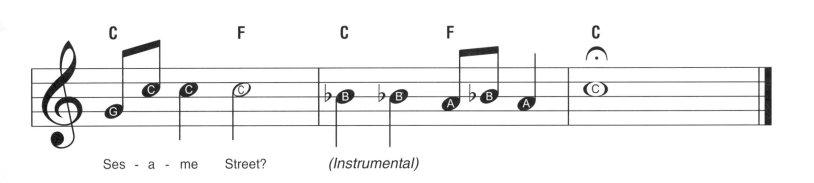

Ses - a - me Street? *(Instrumental)*

Sing
from SESAME STREET

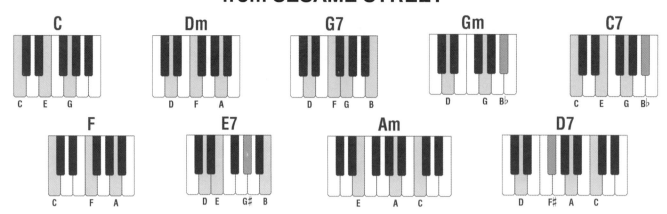

Words and Music by
Joe Raposo

Happily

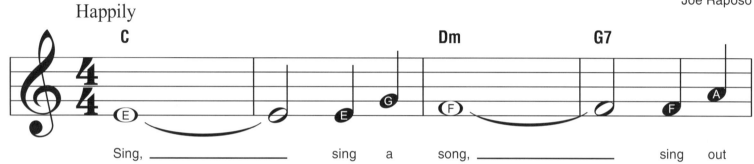

Sing, _____ sing a song, _____ sing out

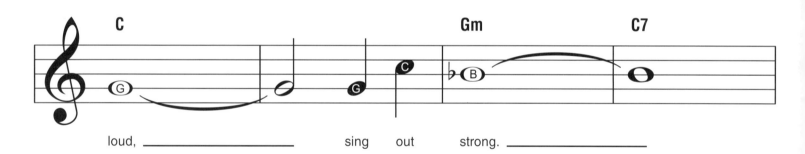

loud, _____ sing out strong. _____

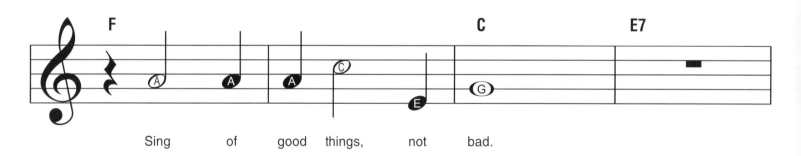

Sing of good things, not bad.

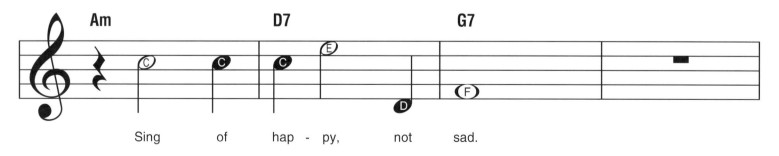

Sing of hap - py, not sad.

So Long, Farewell

from THE SOUND OF MUSIC

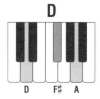

Lyrics by Oscar Hammerstein II
Music by Richard Rodgers

Brightly

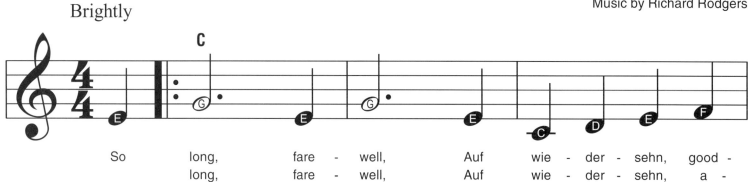

So long, fare - well, Auf wie - der - sehn, good -
long, fare - well, Auf wie - der - sehn, a -

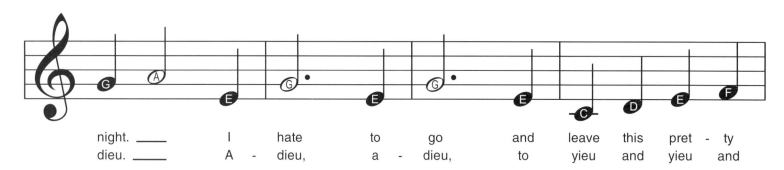

night. _____ I hate to go and leave this pret - ty
dieu. _____ A - dieu, a - dieu, to yieu and yieu and

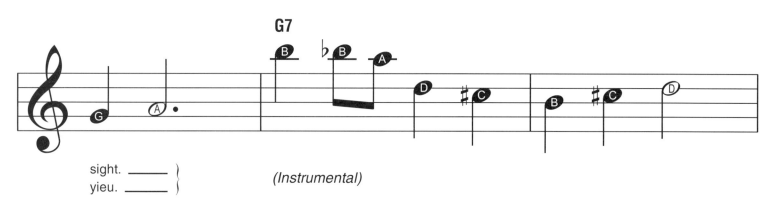

sight. _____ }
yieu. _____ }
(Instrumental)

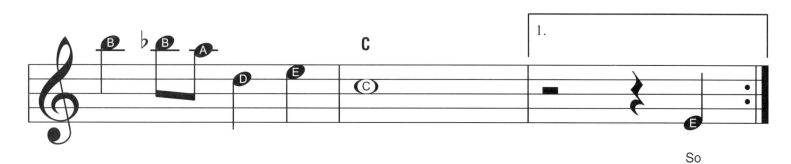

So

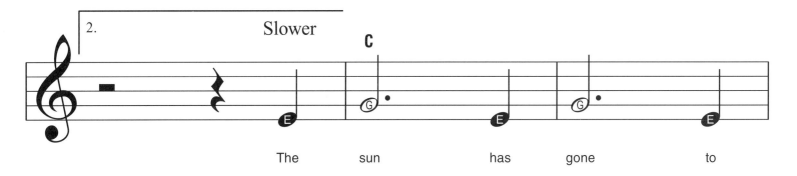

2. Slower

C

The sun has gone to

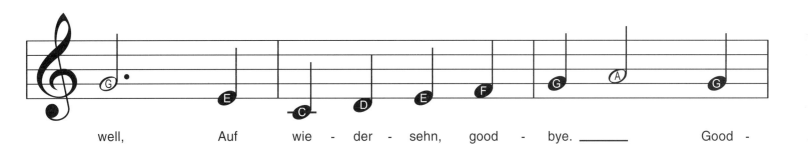

bed and so must I. _____ So long, fare -

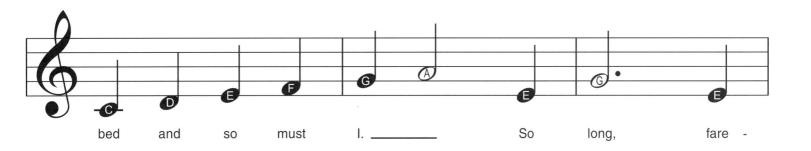

well, Auf - wie - der - sehn, good - bye. _____ Good -

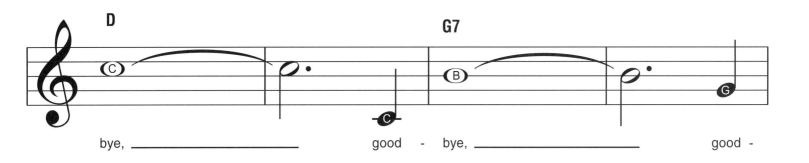

D   G7

bye, _____ good - bye, _____ good -

C

bye, _____ good - bye. _____

Splish Splash

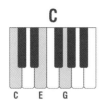
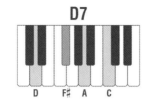
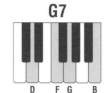
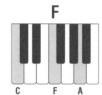

Words and Music by Bobby Darin
and Murray Kaufman

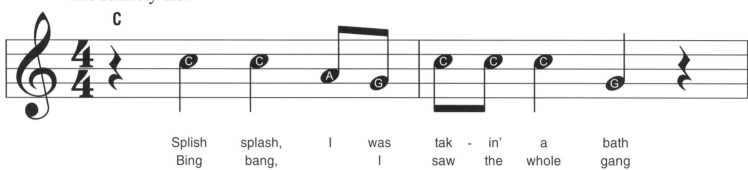

Splish   splash,   I   was   tak - in'   a   bath
Bing   bang,   I   saw   the   whole   gang

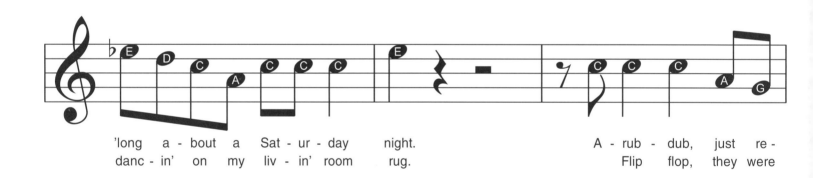

'long   a - bout   a   Sat - ur - day   night.   A - rub - dub,   just   re-
danc - in'   on   my   liv - in'   room   rug.   Flip   flop,   they   were

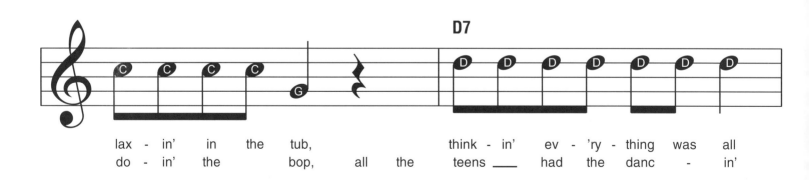

lax - in'   in   the   tub,   think - in'   ev - 'ry - thing   was   all
do - in'   the   bop,   all   the   teens ___ had   the   danc - in'

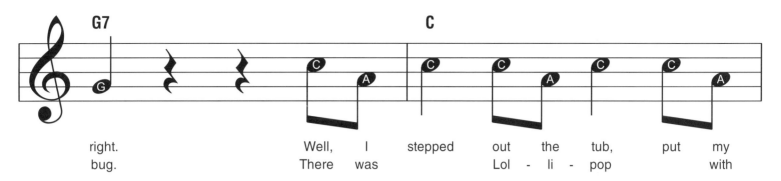

right.
bug.

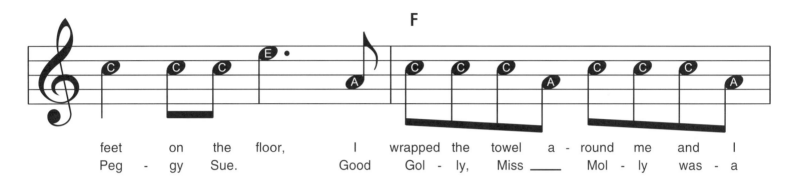

feet on the floor, I wrapped the towel a - round me and I
Peg - gy Sue. Good Gol - ly, Miss ____ Mol - ly was a - a

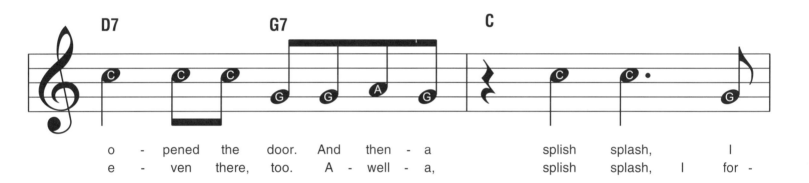

o - pened the door. And then - a splish splash, I
e - ven there, too. A - well - a, splish splash, I for -

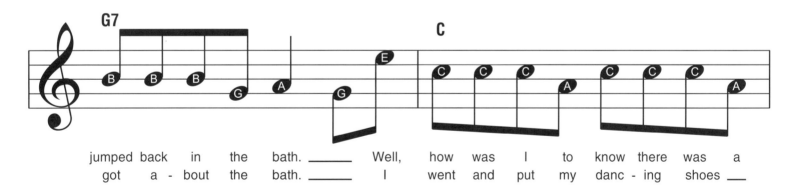

jumped back in the bath. ____ Well, how was I to know there was a
got a - bout the bath. ____ I went and put my danc - ing shoes ___

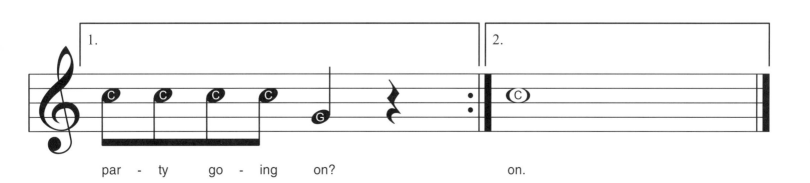

par - ty go - ing on?
on.

SpongeBob SquarePants Theme Song

from SPONGEBOB SQUAREPANTS

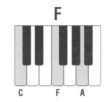

Words and Music by Mark Harrison,
Blaise Smith, Steve Hillenburg
and Derek Drymon

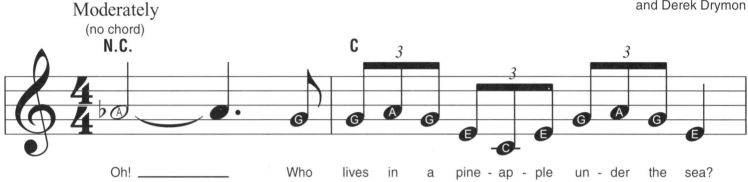

Oh! _____ Who lives in a pine-ap-ple un-der the sea?

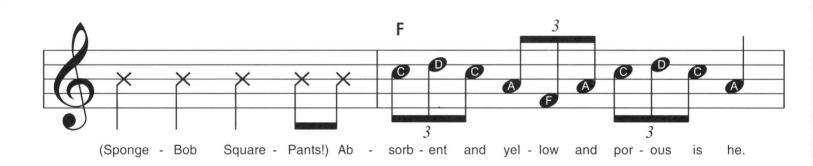

(Sponge-Bob Square-Pants!) Ab-sorb-ent and yel-low and por-ous is he.

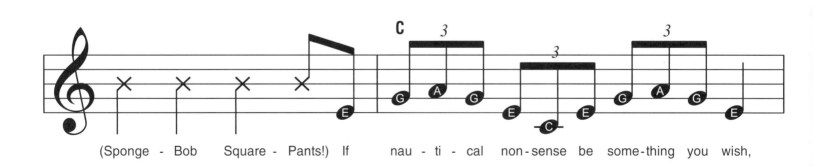

(Sponge-Bob Square-Pants!) If nau-ti-cal non-sense be some-thing you wish,

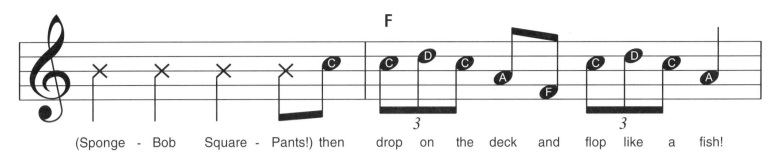

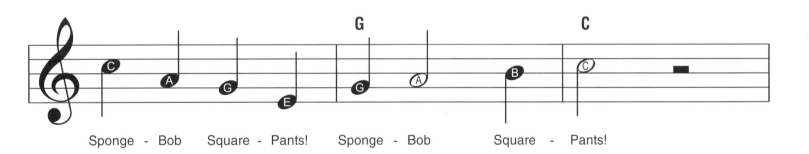

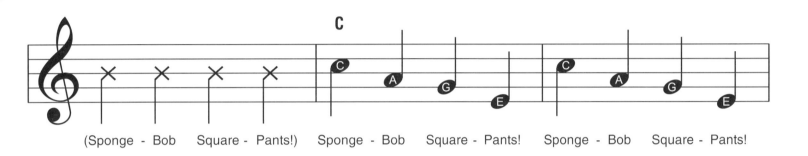

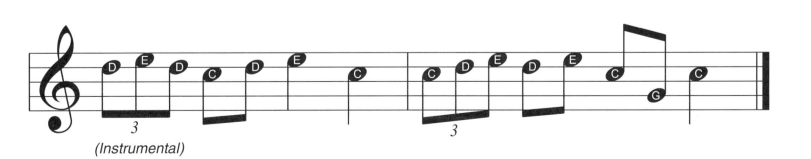

Take Me Out to the Ball Game

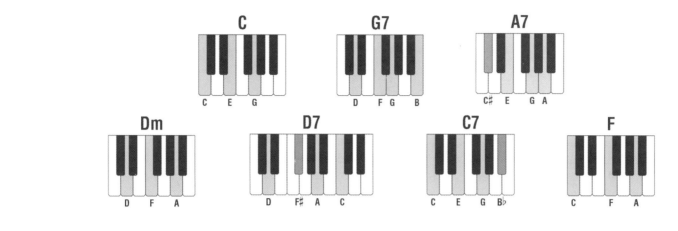

Words by Jack Norworth
Music by Albert von Tilzer

Brightly

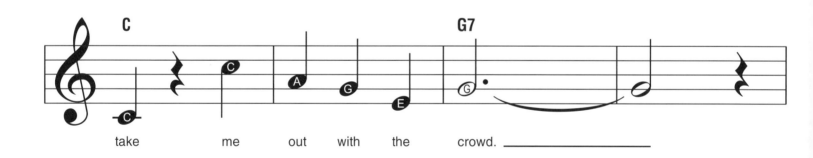

Take me out to the ball game,

take me out with the crowd. _____

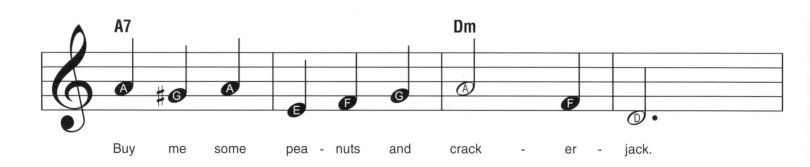

Buy me some pea - nuts and crack - er - jack.

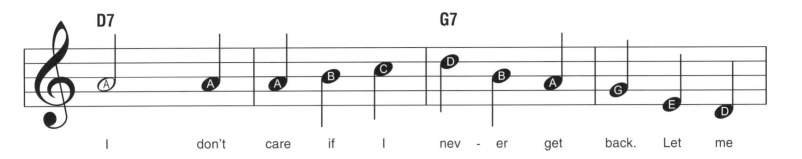

I don't care if I nev-er get back. Let me

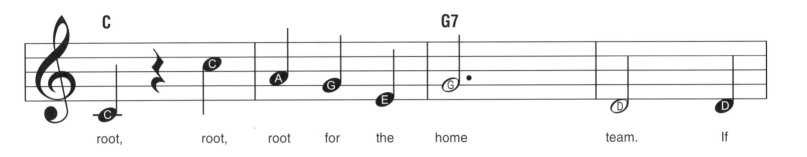

root, root, root for the home team. If

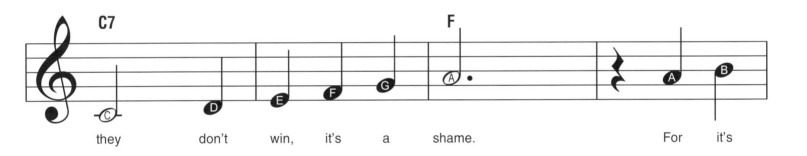

they don't win, it's a shame. For it's

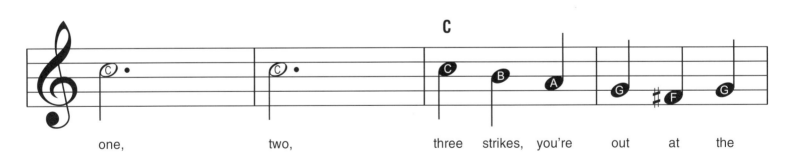

one, two, three strikes, you're out at the

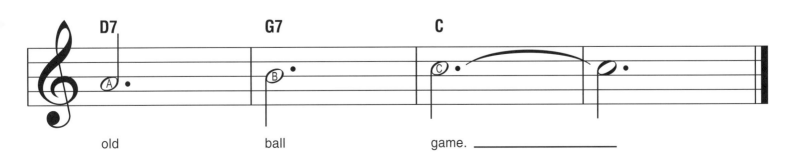

old ball game. _____

This Is My Country

Words by Don Raye
Music by Al Jacobs

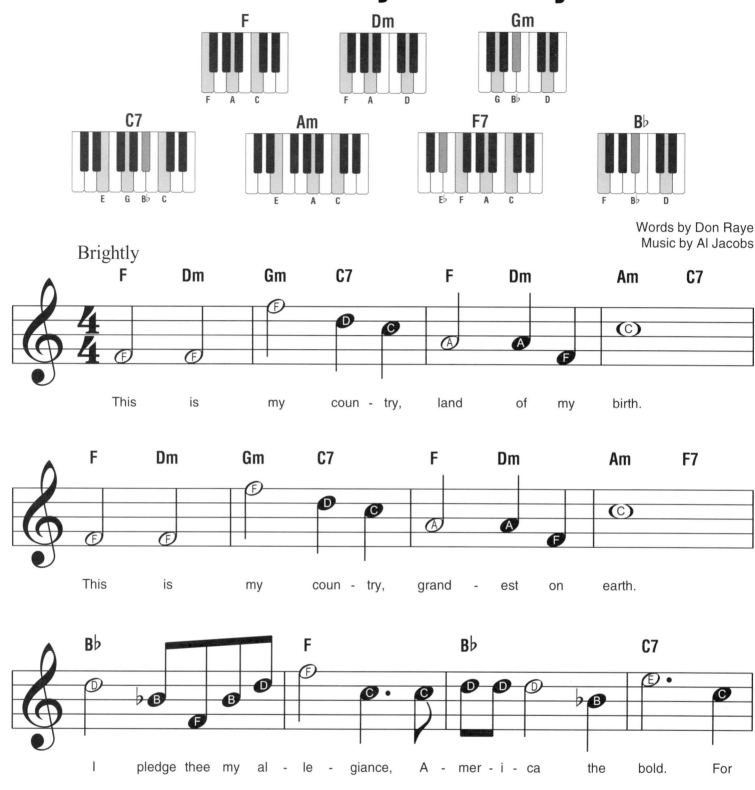

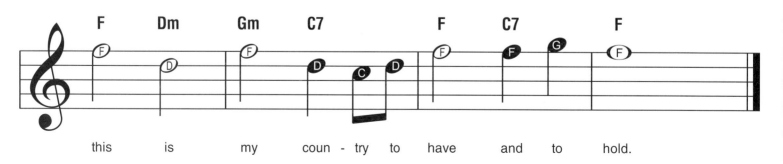

This Land Is Your Land

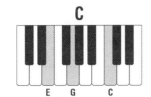
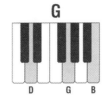
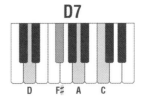

Words and Music by
Woody Guthrie

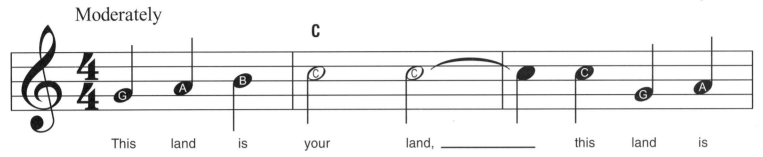

This land is your land, _____ this land is

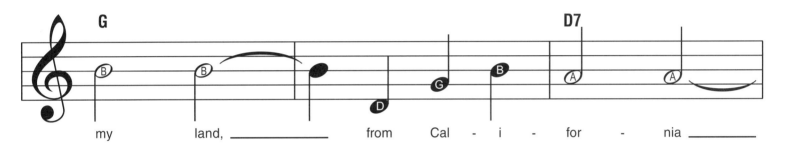

my land, _____ from Cal - i - for - nia _____

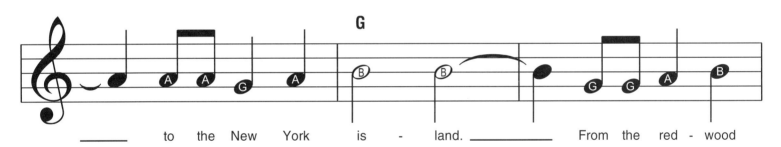

_____ to the New York is - land. _____ From the red - wood

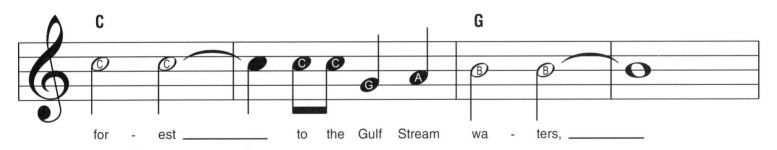

for - est _____ to the Gulf Stream wa - ters, _____

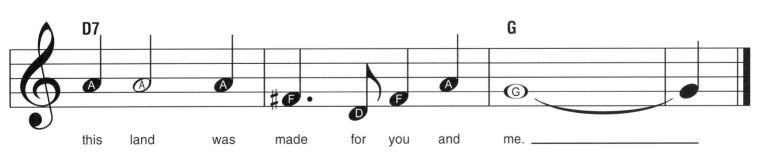

this land was made for you and me. _____

Three Little Birds

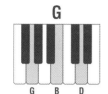 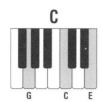 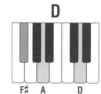 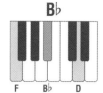

Words and Music by
Bob Marley

Moderate Reggae

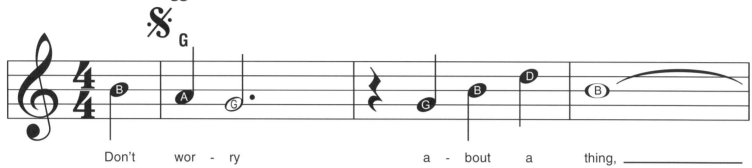

Don't wor - ry   a - bout a   thing, _____

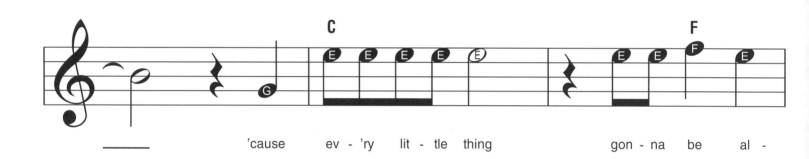

_____ 'cause ev - 'ry lit - tle thing   gon - na be al -

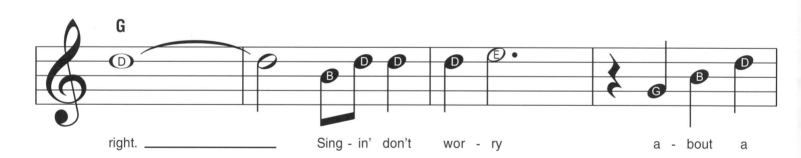

right. _____   Sing - in' don't wor - ry   a - bout a

To Coda

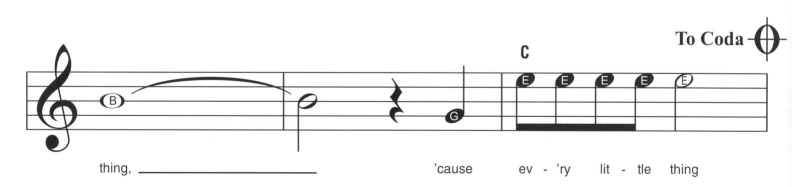

thing, _____   'cause ev - 'ry lit - tle thing

Tomorrow
from the Musical Production ANNIE

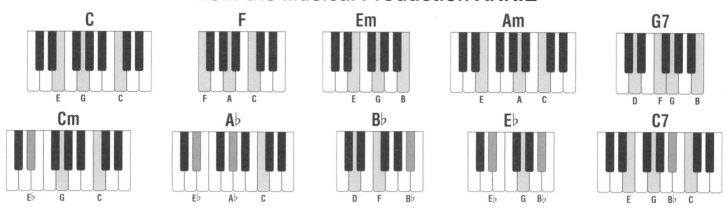

Lyric by Martin Charnin
Music by Charles Strouse

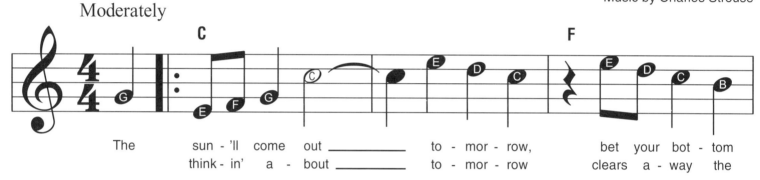

The sun-'ll come out _____ to-mor-row, bet your bot-tom
think-in' a-bout _____ to-mor-row clears a-way the

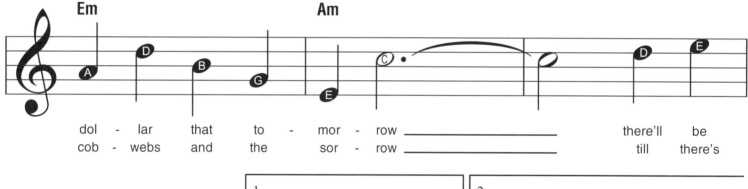

dol-lar that to-mor-row _____ there'll be
cob-webs and the sor-row _____ till there's

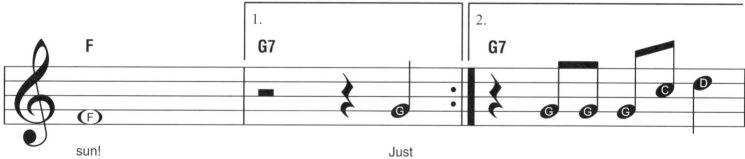

sun!
none.   Just
                              When I'm stuck with a

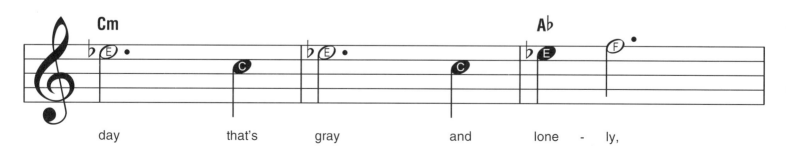

day   that's   gray   and   lone-ly,

Warm Kitty

featured on the CBS Television Show THE BIG BANG THEORY

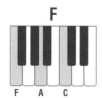
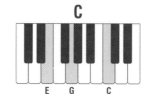
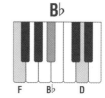

Music adapted from an English Folk Tune by
Laura Pendleton MacCarteney
Lyrics by Edith Newlin

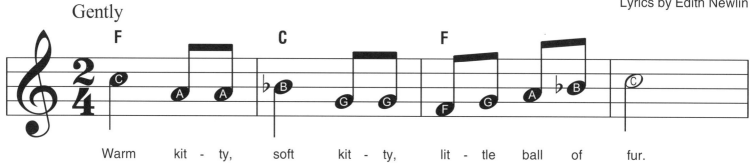

Warm kit - ty, soft kit - ty, lit - tle ball of fur.

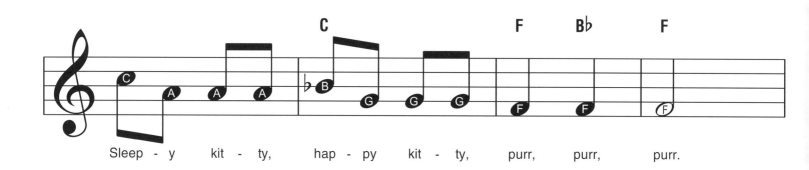

Sleep - y kit - ty, hap - py kit - ty, purr, purr, purr.

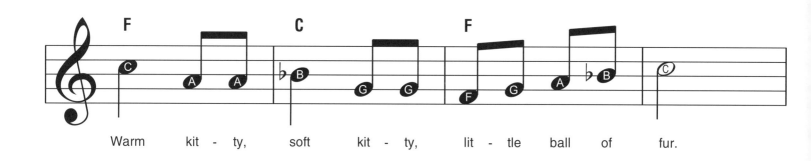

Warm kit - ty, soft kit - ty, lit - tle ball of fur.

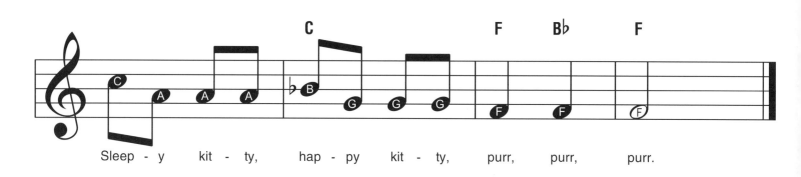

Sleep - y kit - ty, hap - py kit - ty, purr, purr, purr.

The Wheels on the Bus

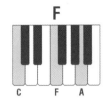
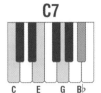

Traditional

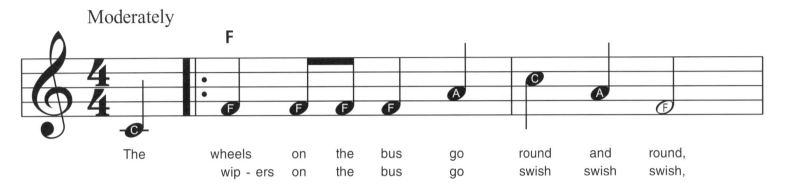

Moderately

The wheels on the bus go round and round,
wip - ers on the bus go round swish and swish swish,

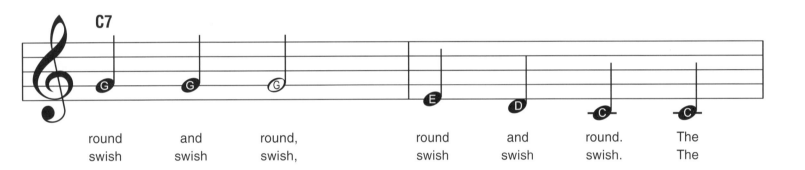

round and round, round and round. The
swish and swish swish, round swish and swish swish. The

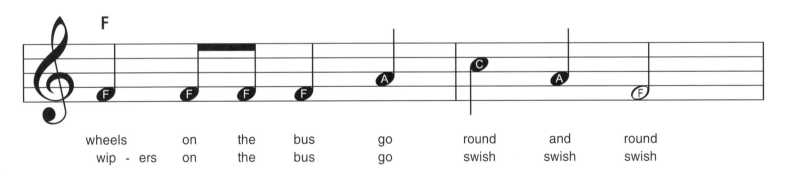

wheels on the bus go round and round
wip - ers on the bus go round swish and swish swish

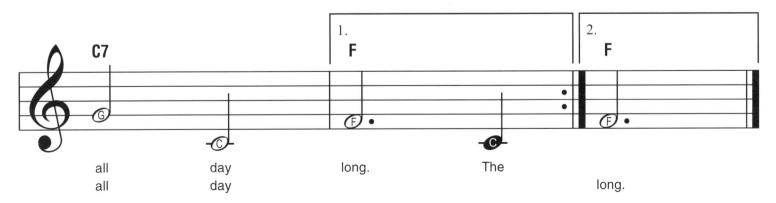

all day long. The
all day long.

We're Off to See the Wizard
from THE WIZARD OF OZ

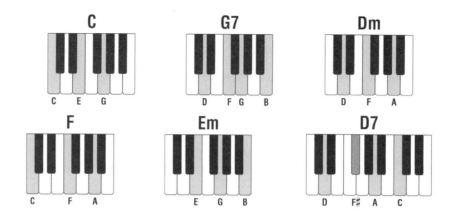

Lyric by E.Y. "Yip" Harburg
Music by Harold Arlen

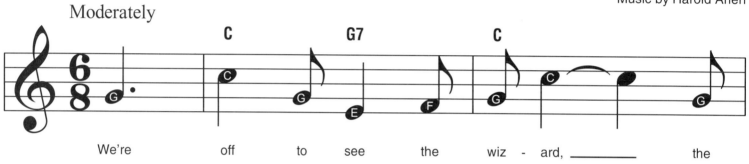

We're off to see the wiz - ard, _____ the

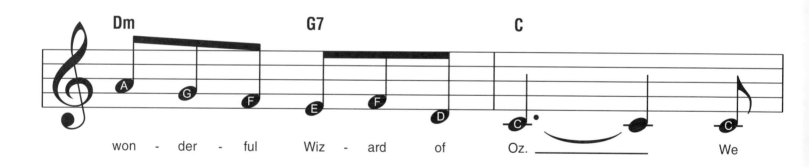

won - der - ful Wiz - ard of Oz. _____ We

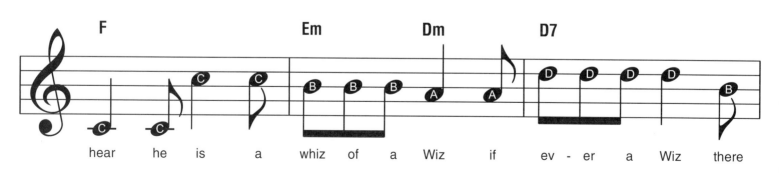

hear he is a whiz of a Wiz if ev - er a Wiz there

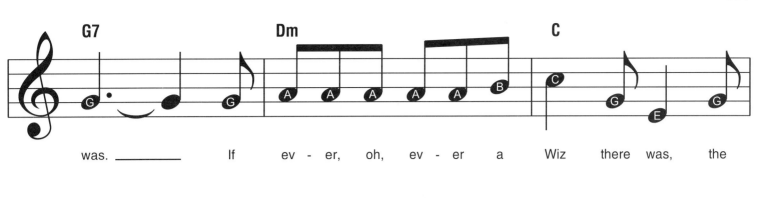

was. _____ If ev - er, oh, ev - er a Wiz there was, the

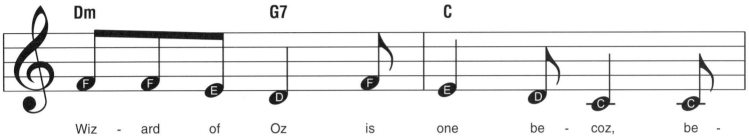

Wiz - ard of Oz is one be - coz, be -

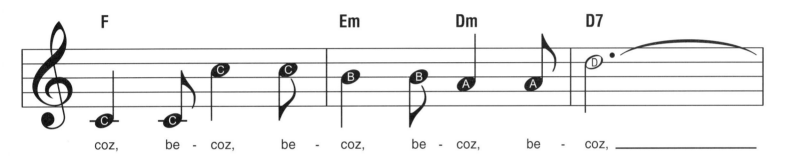

coz, be - coz, be - coz, be - coz, be - coz, _____

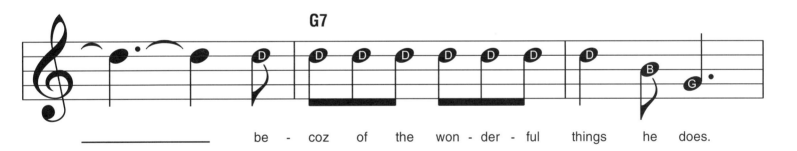

_____ be - coz of the won - der - ful things he does.

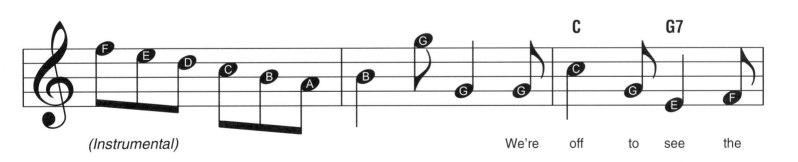

(Instrumental) We're off to see the

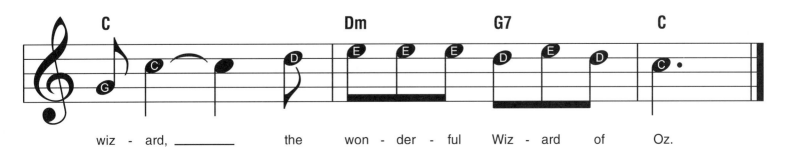

wiz - ard, _____ the won - der - ful Wiz - ard of Oz.

When I Grow Too Old to Dream

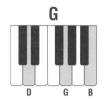
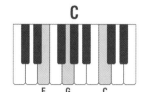
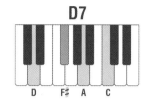
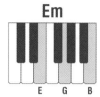
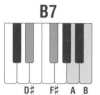

Lyrics by Oscar Hammerstein II
Music by Sigmund Romberg

Moderately

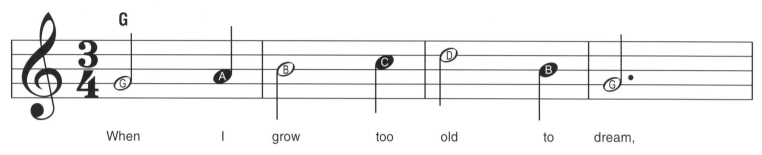

When I grow too old to dream,

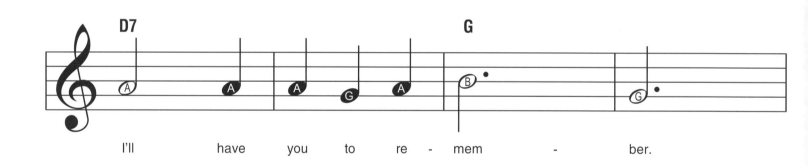

I'll have you to re- mem - ber.

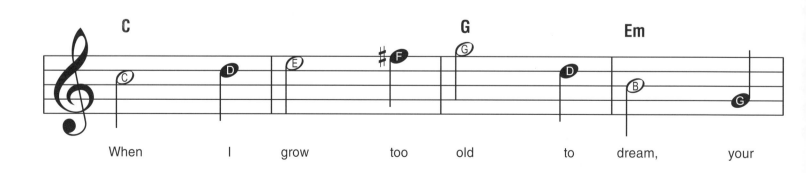

When I grow too old to dream, your

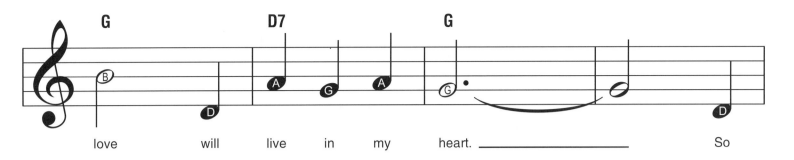

love will live in my heart. _____ So

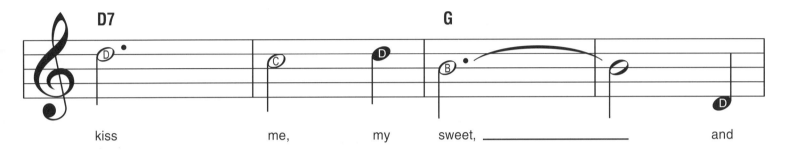

kiss me, my sweet, _____ and

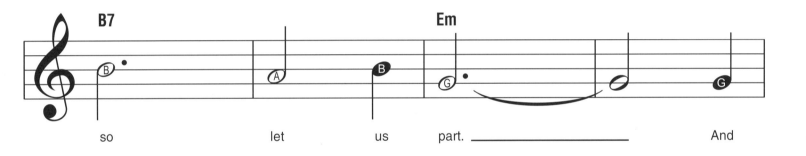

so let us part. _____ And

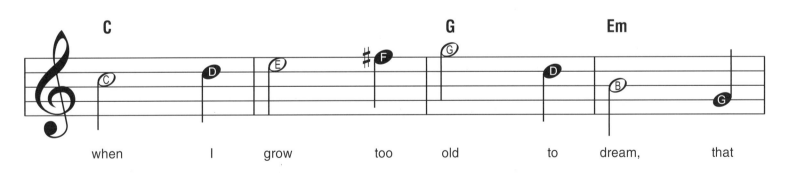

when I grow too old to dream, that

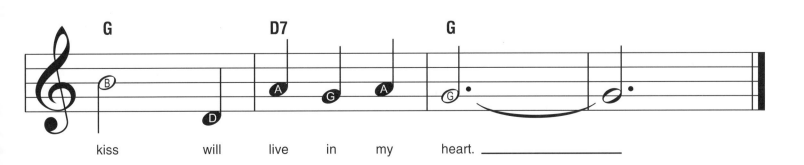

kiss will live in my heart. _____

When I Grow Up
from MATILDA THE MUSICAL

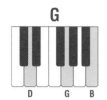
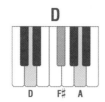
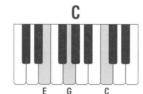
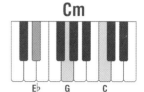

Words and Music by
Tim Minchin

Bright Shuffle

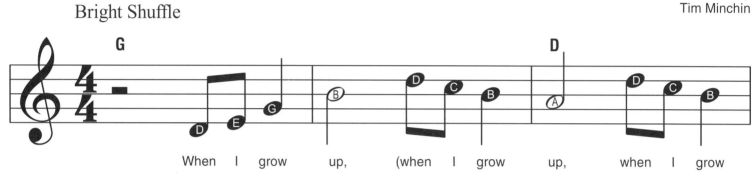

When I grow up, (when I grow up, when I grow

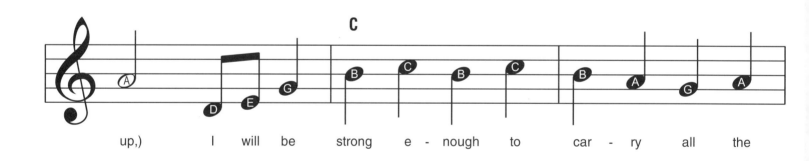

up,) I will be strong e - nough to car - ry all the

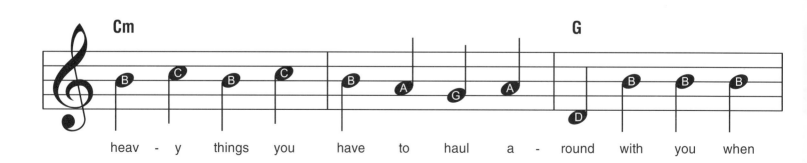

heav - y things you have to haul a - round with you when

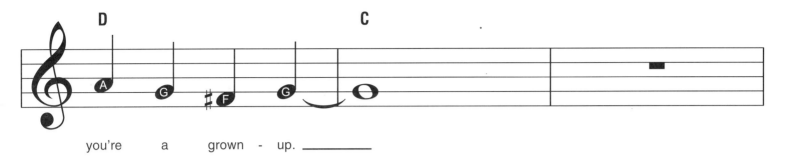

you're a grown - up. _____

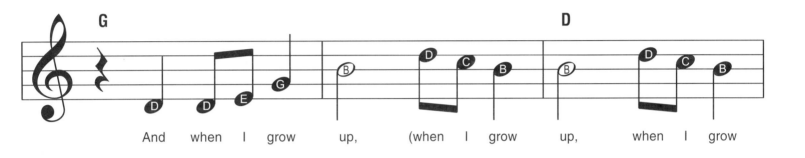

And when I grow up, (when I grow up, when I grow

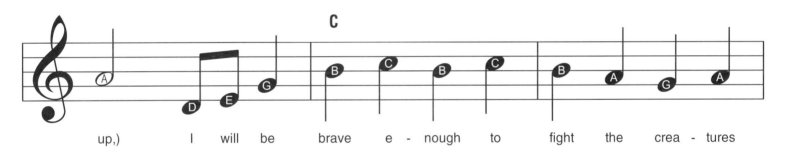

up,) I will be brave e - nough to fight the crea - tures

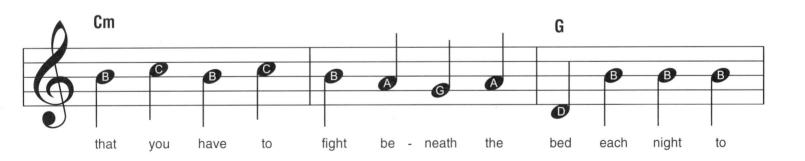

that you have to fight be - neath the bed each night to

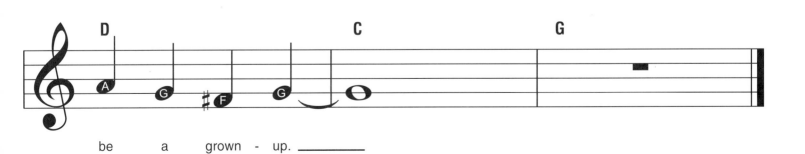

be a grown - up. _____

Where Is Love?

from the Columbia Pictures - Romulus Film OLIVER!

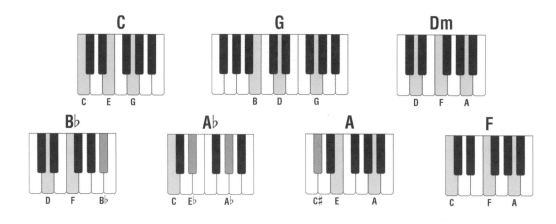

Words and Music by
Lionel Bart

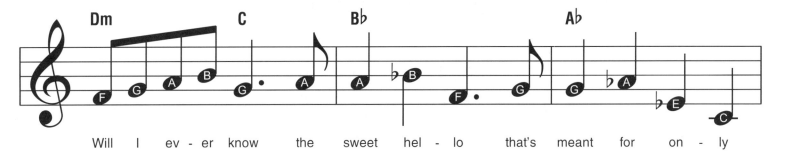

Will I ev - er know the sweet hel - lo that's meant for on - ly

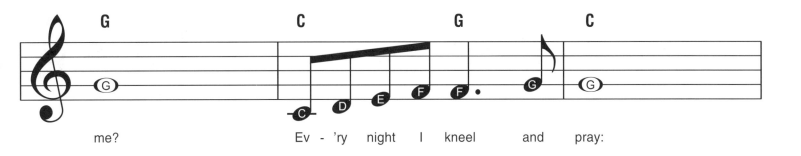

me? Ev - 'ry night I kneel and pray:

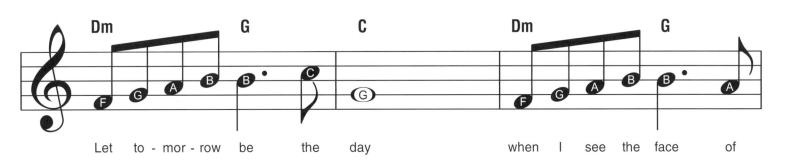

Let to - mor - row be the day when I see the face of

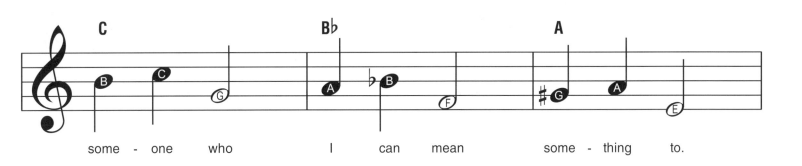

some - one who I can mean some - thing to.

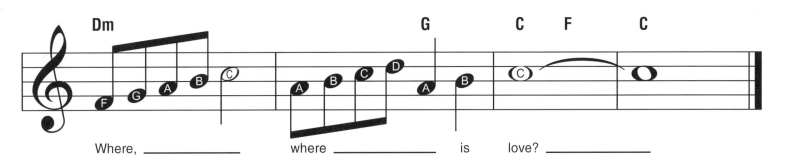

Where, _____ where _____ is love? _____

Won't You Be My Neighbor?

(It's a Beautiful Day in the Neighborhood)
from MISTER ROGER'S NEIGHBORHOOD

Words and Music by
Fred Rogers

You Are My Sunshine

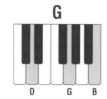
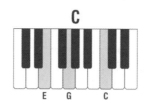
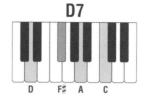

Words and Music by
Jimmie Davis

Moderately

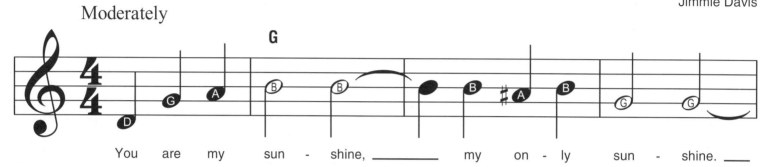

You are my sun - shine, _____ my on - ly sun - shine. __

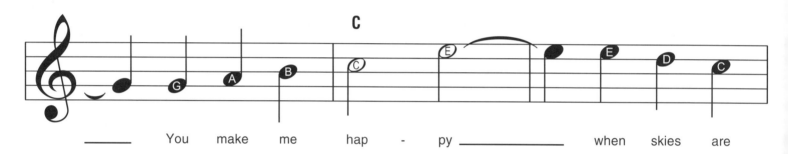

_____ You make me hap - py _____ when skies are

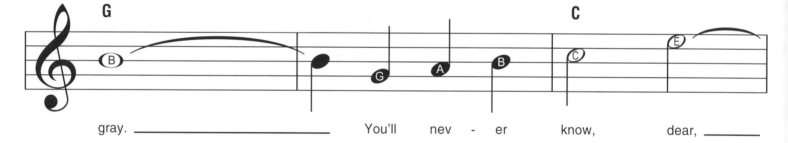

gray. _____ You'll nev - er know, dear, _____

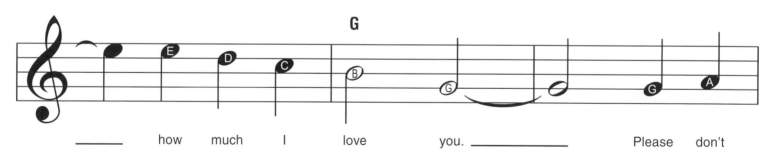

_____ how much I love you. _____ Please don't

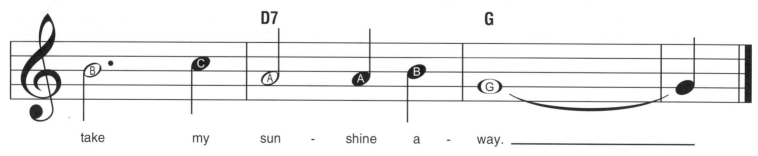

take my sun - shine a - way. _____